Catching Diamonds is a transformational book and treasure trove of charming ideas and activities that are useful and fun for parents, grandparents, and especially anyone involved with children. It is a gift on the path to engaging with children in delightful and meaningful ways to build their imaginations, joy, creativity, self-reliance, and self-respect. These ideas might also be generative for your own life force. I've known Linda for more than 40 years, and she has used and continues to use these ideas in her own life. Intention, light, and laughter have permeated her way of living. We could all benefit from a little more of that in our lives.

~ GRAY MANNAKEE
Entrepreneur & Writer

When I was a child, I was lucky to have adults in my life, especially my grandmothers, who gave me their precious time and attention. While reading Linda's beautiful book on fun and easy ways to be fully present with children, I recognized the beautiful gift of their love, time spent with me, and how special I felt when I was with them. I am now a mother myself of a two-year-old, Krew, and I am so happy to have Catching Diamonds as a guide to help me have diverse fun and increased imaginative and playful times with my own child. Reading *Catching Diamonds*, I am reminded of so many moments shared with my grandmothers—easy moments, everyday moments of magical connections. I hope that *Catching Diamonds* finds its way into every home so that we can all be reminded of what gifts we can be for each other.

~ CAMILLE DURBIN
Mother of two-year-old Krew

This book is a literary magical mystery tour for engaging children and developing imaginations. And like any good magical mystery tour, one should always have it handy when the impulse to delve into expansive and imaginary realms strikes. *Catching Diamonds* opens doors we've forgotten about and hands us a roadmap of streets that have faded into distant memory. The wonder of life is always there to be seen and felt. Thank goodness we have this book to remind us of that!

~ THOMAS WISELEY, MD
and grandfather of four

Catching Diamonds

*Fostering Imagination and Creating
Enchantment with the Children in
Your Life, and with Yourself*

Linda Fleischhauer Collins

WITH ILLUSTRATIONS BY
Jim Collins

Cover design © 2021 by Eric Finstad, AD Creative Group and Jim Collins, Concept Designs

Original artwork © 2021 Jim Collins

Editorial consultant: Elaine Silver

Book design: Carl Brune

Website: catchingdiamonds.com

Published by Know Where Land (knowwhereland.com)

ISBN 978-1-7375916-0-3

This book is dedicated to my mother,
Clara Suzanne McFarland Fleischhauer

She planted seeds of curiosity, imagination, laughter, and wonder that are growing strong now and will flower in many generations to come.

She lived in the wisdom of love, protection, gratitude and joy for all those she encountered.

TABLE OF CONTENTS

PART 5

ADULTS NEED TO PLAY, TOO

POSTSCRIPT

NOTES

I met Linda Collins when I was pregnant with my daughter, Coco, and I've had the privilege to be Linda's friend for more than 30 years since. As my daughter was growing up, Linda was instrumental in helping bring imagination and creative play into Coco's young life. Like a duck to water, Coco fully embraced imaginative play, like the idea that fairies and leprechauns were her secret friends and that the autumn ground was covered in glowing paint left by mischievous wee ones. Linda tutored her in the fine art of seeing sparkling life all around her.

If not for Linda's support and guidance, I could not have given my daughter the same experience of rich, inspired creativity that she had in childhood. And the creative outlook Linda fostered in that childhood has continued into adulthood. Because Linda is so naturally geared to being imaginative, it is truly infectious for those of us around her. I'm so pleased to be able to now support Linda in her endeavor to spread her gifts to a wider audience with this book.

My professional career as executive coach, management consultant, author, and trainer in the field of positive human and organizational change gives me a unique perspective on how imagination, or vision, and positive focus help people grow into the best version of themselves. This is what Linda nurtures in the children she connects with—a strong belief in their inner capacity to blossom under the right guidance and encouragement.

Children are individually unique, and each child has the potential to grow and develop into a well-functioning and playful adult—unless they do not have access to the social, economic, cultural, and familial advantages that foster such growth. Linda's book helps address that gap by offering a myriad of suggestions to help children truly be able to engage in positive and inventive play. Most of Linda's ideas can be implemented at no cost, making them accessible to anyone reading this book. She also wants to touch adults who may not have been raised with or exposed to ways of seeing the world in the way she does, which is through the lens of spontaneity, beauty, adventure, and sheer potential. Many of us might not know how to access that in ourselves and are limited in how we can do that for the children in our lives. Linda's book speaks to us adults as well, encouraging us with another chance in life to grow and learn.

Linda herself has used her gifts professionally in her role as a case manager, supporting her seriously ill and disabled clients in seeing the beauty around them, no matter how challenging the circumstances.

It is a true gift to be able bring light into the world around you. I am so happy that Linda's brightness can now reach so many more of us.

~ ANN L. CLANCY, PH.D.
Author of Appreciative *Coaching: A Positive Process for Change*
May 2021

Over the years, many of my friends and family members, have asked me to help them bring more of the enchantment of the moment into their interactions with their children and grandchildren. They started calling for me to write a book. I shared my stories, ideas, and suggestions with them, but they wanted a book they could take home with them to refer to in a moment's notice, or to give as a gift to a new parent or grandparent. I wanted to write that book, but it was not something I had done before. I had no idea how it could actually happen. So, I sent out the wish, intention, and desire for a way forward to creating this book from both a parental and professional point of view. I opened myself up to enchantment and to mystery and watched to see what happened.

In the spring of 2018, I took an unusual journey to Mexico City and the ancient temple site of Teotihuacan. This was not like any trip I had taken before. I went with a group of three of my good friends. We joined up with a larger group with a very knowledgeable guide who led us through the ancient ruins and the vibrant, life-enhancing energies that still swirl around Teotihuacan. One of our adventures was to the Basilica of Our Lady of Guadalupe, the Church of Miracles, in Mexico City. People all over Mexico and Central and South America revere Our Lady of Guadalupe as the one who ended the violence against the native people after the Spanish arrived in the Americas. Her Basilica is truly a place of miracles and magic, and many pilgrims come to visit.

After leaving the Basilica, my mind and heart were immediately captivated by the vast, colorful beauty and abundant energy of Mexico City on that brilliantly sunny day. I had almost forgotten the fact that moments before I had said a heartfelt prayer asking that I get a sign about writing this book—or a sign if I needed to let the idea go.

Within two minutes after leaving the church, I started walking with one of the members of our group. The first question out of my mouth to her was, "Do you work inside the home or out of it?" I know, what an unusual question this was to immediately ask someone that you are just getting to know, but it popped right out of my mouth.

"Well," she replied, "I am an editor, writer, and journalist."

I couldn't believe what I was hearing. I had just asked for a sign and there it was, standing right next to me. I immediately launched into my story. I told her, "I feel like I'm supposed to write this book, but I have never written one. I'm a bit overwhelmed by the idea of this process." I was really just being honest and in awe that she was the one who happened to start walking next to me.

With a smiling, angelic face, she looked at me and said, "That is exactly what I do. I help people create and edit their books."

With a new lightness and a great feeling of support around the idea of this book materializing, I looked straight back at her, and simply said, "You are my Miracle!" We started working together in May of 2019. And now you are holding the book in your hands—if that is not magic, I don't know what is!

When children and adults together build imaginative, interactive worlds, everyone involved receives the gift of expansiveness and belonging to a community where they are seen, heard, protected, and loved. These are also miracles in my mind.

As this book unfolded, not only did it take the direction of supporting interactions between adults and children, but it also became a reference for adults expanding their ways of interacting within their own worlds while supporting themselves in our fast-paced world of roles and demands.

The sharing in this book is a combination of interactions with children and others in my life, educational and work experience, personal experiences, and just from life itself. This is the type of book you can enjoy reading from cover to cover or picking and choosing as your interests lead you. It can be a reference book for ideas for interacting, playing, and creating experiences with children. The stories and enchantments are written for children to hear and enjoy.

INTRODUCTION

I believe one of the reasons others were so eager to broaden their knowledge of playful interactions with children is the promise these exchanges will include refreshing sprinkles of joy and delight without complicated rules, and, generally, involve little planning. These types of connections with children can be explored anywhere— from vibrant, individual moments to captivating hours to absorbing days of liveliness and sharing. The stories and ideas in this book can help enhance memories, teachings, and all-consuming pleasure and laughter. They are heart-rich! This type of play is there for anyone. All you need is an open heart and a good-natured imagination.

What exactly am I talking about? What are these magical times with children? They are the times when your attention, your imagination, and your love are in sync with a child's attention, imagination, and love. They are the times when you are treating the child as a unique and beautiful expression of themselves. They are the times when you are appreciating the gift that child is to you and to the whole world. They are the times of collaboration. They are the times of unexpected outcomes. They are the times when you take off your "must do" hat and put on your "fun do" one. They are the times when you really see the spirit of the young one. They are the times when you remember the young one that you once were and still are.

The beauty and essence of this book is encouraging adults and children to spend time together wrapped in experiences that touch hearts and build supportive connections while creating rich memories and learning in conscious moments which can include your own rich culture's lore and imaginings. In this book, I have included stories, wisdom and adventures with the elves and fairies which were part of my experiences and folklore of playfulness growing up. I have continued to pass the joy of these imaginings on to my children and grandchildren. You can pass on the stories you value and bring you joy from your own history, just as I have.

Please note that this lore is compatible and not exclusive with learning about things scientifically, which are also included in this book. The richness of imagination and scientific knowledge go hand-in-hand in developing a deep curiosity and enthusiasm for the richness and potency of connection in the worlds around us.

This book is about creating these times by:

Helping instill in children a solid sense of creativity, self-esteem, and wonder.

Helping you get in touch with your inner child, youthful self, and stories from your own childhood.

Reminding you of the beauty you're already creating. You will find that you are already engaging in many of these elements and ways of being with your children, others, and yourself that are described in this book. This book is a reminder for you to stop and appreciate yourself and all you contribute to life and to those around you.

Be on the lookout throughout the book for "ENCHANTMENT ALERTS." These words tell you that we are going right into the imaginative scene—a land of pretend—fully engaged with the moment and the scenario that's being presented. This approach is a portal into another way of seeing the world and a different way to use our senses. By evoking your own Enchantment Alerts, like by including the ideas of elves and fairies or the playful characters from your own specific culture's legends and lore, you are signaling to yourself and to the child that you are on high alert for beauty and wonder. And that you are willing to fully focus on the world around you for those moments. Plus, you are also creating a specific shared reality with the child. It is an agreed upon way to see the world at that moment. This agreement creates a special community between you and the child. And that special community is where real connection can occur.

Here is the first ENCHANTMENT ALERT:

Elves and Fairies ENCHANTMENT ALERT!: You will
note as you read through the book that my imagination
leads me down the path to the magical realm of elves,
fairies, and other elusive creatures living among us. In
fact, throughout the years, the most frequent request
that I get from those who know about the way elves and
fairies appear in my interactions with the children in my
life is to explain how they too can make these delightful
creatures appear in their lives. Now, here's the thing:
there is no forcing it. Either the elves and fairies appeal
to you and it makes sense to you to invite them into your
world, or there is something else that awaits you such as
a secret pal or friend. Either way, in the infinite expanse
of imaginative play, there are scenarios available to suit
you and the children around you. The imaginative world
that you build with a child will be as unique as the
individuals that you all are.

What if children learn how to be positive and comfortable
with their abilities to brainstorm for the best possible outcome
to any question or problem early in their growing lives? My
experience is if children have been encouraged, guided, and
supported in learning life skills through the loving attention of the
adults in their lives, they will innately use those skills throughout
their lives. So, as important as the joy that these encounters
bring, is the extra benefit that children can playfully acquire
important skills and patterns that will allow them to tap into the
"Fountain of Youth" throughout their entire lives. Being lively and
enveloped in the treasures of life are natural inclinations of the
young. Being able to nurture and reinforce these natural abilities
is a privilege for those of us who get to spend time with children.
These positive ways of navigating life are sought after in dealing
with work, activities, friendships, and romantic relationships.
They can be utilized in all aspects of life. Children who have the
gift of imagination and awareness learn how to creatively work
past their fears and refine positive habits. These varied abilities

support them in working towards their own dreams and how they want their lives to be, to feel, and to unfold. They won't settle for just existing as they grow; they will innately and naturally be drawn to creating a harmony in their lives that brings them back to the peace and wholeness they learned and felt as children. They will live more internally motivated versus being more externally motivated. What better gifts could you arrange for the children in your life as they are accumulating and refining their toolbox of life skills?

So, while you are having a great time exploring imaginative realms with the children in your life, you will also be teaching them how to support themselves in good times as well as difficult times.

You will be reading stories of some memories from my childhood with my mom, and times with my children, grandchildren, and others in my life. And, yes, playful descriptions of elves and fairies, as well as encouragement for you to engage with these enchanting beings, will be sprinkled throughout these pages. Many of you will have seen the "I Spy"-type books where there are hidden objects in the pictures. Well, this book is similar, but instead of hidden objects, you will be looking for hidden ways of increasing the richness of adventures and time spent together with children, others, and yourselves.

To deepen your involvement with these stories, look for clues signaling when you feel your heart is touched. If you are inspired to imagine a scene or idea unfolding, you are meeting the challenge of finding clues. You will know you are on the right track if you find yourself thinking you would like to explore, learn, or jump into the moment. (Be on the lookout for those "Enchantment Alerts!" which herald a moment of playful imagination.) I hope your curiosity is stirred and you can't resist exploring some of your own twists and takes on learning and connection.

Pop into these stories with a full heart while involving all of your senses, and bring their feeling cousins along to create an even fuller picture.

(Oh, and don't forget to keep a stack of sticky notes next to you while you are reading. You can mark places in the book that you want to revisit and you can jot down ideas you have for fun activities.)

Adults are here to help children maintain the awe and freshness of living in moments while encouraging their independence and maturing selves. The best scientific research that you can read about this subject is still just second-hand information. This book is about a living experiment, about self-inquiry and self-discovery. There is no substitute for one's own observation. My 45-plus years of experience with children shows me that inspiring a healthy curiosity in children at a young age will equip them in the fullest of ways to be imaginative and grounded in their own lives as they grow. Some think imagination and creativity are not the most important skills to acquire. Those people may feel they fall under the headings of frivolous, flighty, irresponsible, or not having a sense of purpose or value. If these are some impressions that come to mind for you, I hope you will test that theory by doing your own investigative experiments and see what results you get.

The following list will give you a taste of the ideas in this book. This book is about:

🍃 Discovering how imagination and creativity can happen anywhere.

🍃 Developing an increased sense of purpose, enjoying your capabilities, exploring potential to encourage a youthful spirit that is maintained and refined into adulthood. Keeping a genuine sense of anticipation and hope into adulthood. Understanding the importance of cultivating and weaving a sense of wonder into one's life, which includes valuing a sense of adventure and play.

🍃 Helping children who are curiously learning to question and educate themselves. Being a doer rather than just a watcher. Being both an inspired leader and an enthusiastic student. Becoming a bit of a detective when looking for new ideas and possibilities.

Building a solid go-to support system beginning with parents and grandparents. Gaining interests which can be healthy coping skills and supports. Learning and finetuning skills of patience, positivity, and resilience.

Learning how to put ideas, dreams, needs, and possibilities out there, and move towards them as they move towards you. Developing perseverance in achieving goals. Seeing wider visions of ways to engage in and create one's life.

Understanding the connectedness and appreciation of the vast environments around us and in the world. Learning to understand and appreciate difference and diversity in people, life, and our worlds.

Learning to entertain ourselves in active ways versus always being entertained.

Cultivating humor and lightheartedness.

Learning how choices create consequences while knowing outcomes can be positive or negative.

Turning the ordinary into extraordinary. Finding joy and richness around every corner are real treasures in life.

Being comfortable with the idea of challenging ourselves without the assurance of known outcomes; in other words, taking a leap in faith in trying new ideas, interests, and directions. A good part of a new adventure is in the creativeness, anticipation, and the journey. With this approach, the idea of fear, anxiety, or self-judgements dissipate as the experience becomes about engagement rather than perfection or mastery. This leads to the genuine peacefulness of the world being wide open to explore in our own ways.

PART 1

STORIES OF IMAGINATION
AND ENCHANTMENT

CHAPTER 1

THE BASIC RECIPE

Imagination is, of course, one of the cornerstones of stepping into the fountain of youthful enchantment. You may find yourself capturing the charming spiritedness of enchantment quite easily.

Seeing beyond the material world into the magic everywhere around us!

> STEP 1: Decide that the time you wish to share with the child in your life is conscious time, time where you will be present—even if it is for just a few minutes.
>
> STEP 2: Add in curiosity and creativity.
>
> STEP 3: Stir with delighting in and celebrating the world that you create.
>
> STEP 4: Let the adventures of youthful play begin.
>
> Youthful play—doesn't that seem like some antiquated notion? Our young people are barely given a moment to get used to the world before being asked to repair it. I say the place to start the repair is to first let our children have a sense of magic and miracles of this wondrous world we live in. Let them have a sense of infinite possibilities while remembering possibilities are truly infinite. The sky is the limit in terms of gifts for both adults and children when we enter into the unexpected in the present moment.

A sense of imagination and the ability to look beyond the everyday world were gifts my mother gave to me. She saw many moments as invitations to ignite her own imagination as well as her children's. She used imagination as a way to connect to us and have us connect to each other and to ourselves—creating a fun and adventurous shared reality. She would talk some about elves and fairies and other magical characters like Jack Frost. We would spend intriguing moments lying in the soft green grass watching the changeable clouds circle above us, seeing their bountiful energy and ability to change forms right before our eyes. It was always a great game to see if we could see the same creature in the clouds as the next person.

One of the last times I remember Mom giving the gift of her imagination was when part of our family was riding in my brother's boat on Flathead Lake in Montana on a beautiful summer's day. My brother and I were already well into adulthood, and my mother was in her late seventies. The boat was clipping along at a high speed while bouncing across the water. Shimmering water droplets cascaded all around us. As the water and sun danced intricately together, my mom reached her hand out. ENCHANTMENT ALERT! She was extracting handfuls of imaginary diamonds which she gently and playfully placed in our outstretched hands. At that point, we were all laughing with the gift of lightheartedness and sharing the wealth of merriment. I believe all of us felt in those moments that we had been offered something much richer than a handful of valuable gems.

You may have already experienced many plentiful gifts of imagination. Even if you haven't, it won't take you long to learn how to bring fascination into moments with children, yourself, and others. These adventures may be a bit like getting in touch with your own playful self that oftentimes gets buried in the worlds of adulthood and responsibilities.

Do you remember the days when you would wake up with the anticipation of how each day was going to unfold? What bountifulness were you going to cook up in your exuberance? Who were you going to play with? What surprises might be around the corner? Who will come to visit? What might show up in the mail? What book might drop into your life? What will happen at school? When the neighborhood awakens, what stories of adventure and intrigue might be written for that day?

If you don't remember this feeling upon waking—whether you never have experienced it or you have forgotten it—you can gradually make it a part of your morning consciousness. It is just a thought away! Many of the suggestions in the book will help you gain or regain this excitement.

So, your adult self might think it is just another day, but to an energetic, youthful soul waking from a peaceful night's slumber, there are elements of anticipation for the day of surprises, connections, and mysteries that are awaiting, seemingly randomly, to drop into the richness of the day. The young are committed with all their might and energy to exploring life and its moments. They intuitively connect with the whole of themselves. They do this from the abundance of feelings they experience, the symphony of sounds they hear, the exploration of touch they engage in, the flavors they exuberantly taste, and the never-ending journey of what they see and imagine. This is a mighty full and well-stocked pantry to start baking their worlds of infinite possibilities.

There are many messages we hear and read about being fully present and living life with a richness and connectedness in moments. Your complete attention is your gift to yourself in truly being alive. When most of us come across these brilliant, inspirational ideas, we can feel we have been touched by the refreshingly angelic lure of turning ordinary moments, as the sayings promise, into magnificent, almost magical ways of being. We have a yearning for ordinary moments to be filled with this richness. We plan with great gusto to integrate these alluring ideas into our lives. But they oftentimes seemingly fade away as our bustling lives call us back to our now realities with or without us really knowing we just lost a bit of the magic of life itself.

I believe this deep and beautiful yearning, in part, is simply a remembering by our unconscious minds of how we were when we were young, and a desire to replicate the simplicity and intricacy of younger days while having full-bodied experiences with ease. Remembering what it was like to be young and fully involved in the present moment is the first step in being able to truly engage with a child. We have to walk into their world rather than ask them to conform to ours. By doing so, we give them the acknowledgment that we see what their world is like. Think Peter Pan and his Lost Boys or Christopher Robin and his Winnie-the-Pooh.

Along these lines of memories, two years ago, my son and daughter came to town together without their families and called to see if I was available for dinner. When we were at dinner, the strangest and most startling memories of feelings passed by and through me. I felt transported back to the times when we all three lived together for all of those years. I was flooded with how happy we were in the time we shared, how easy it has continued to be over time, and how much I loved them. I was truly overwhelmed by this gift of reflection. I looked at them with happy tears in my eyes, and said, "It felt like I literally went all the way back in time to when you were younger." I was in awe of the realness of my feelings. I said, "We were so happy, weren't we? It was so easy with the three of us!" And they fully agreed.

I challenge you to close your eyes and go back in time to a seemingly ordinary moment that is etched in your storage bank of memory. Take your time and make it as real as the day it happened. Enjoy the smiles and memories tucked in your own heart. We will be exploring this idea of conjuring scenes, both from memories and from our imaginations, throughout the book. So, give it a whirl and see what you come up with now; but don't worry, you will have lots of opportunity to practice.

CHAPTER 2

MY MOTHER'S GIFTS

In these next parts, I share memories and stories from my life. Please, as you go on these journeys into the realm of imagination and enchantment, listen with an anticipating spirit in your heart. Each of these stories is designed to remind you to awaken those parts of yourself which used to regularly engage in flights of imagination. The stories are designed to inspire you to make your reservations to take those flights again with the young ones in your life.

SENSORY MEMORIES

The first memory that just popped into my head happened when I was about six years old:

A Duck, Watermelon, and Three Energetic Children

The scene is our backyard where my dad had built a pen for our beautiful, energetic pet duck, Donald. Mom sent us out the back door to Donald's pen with a cascading plate of luscious watermelon. We headed barefoot outside to the pen and squished ourselves together on a handmade wooden bench. The watermelon seemed to methodically disappear as we joyfully fed ourselves and Donald. The light red juice was sticky as it dripped sleepily down our arms. The duck was vivaciously quacking and dancing from one side of the pen to the other as we spit watermelon seeds and threw rinds into his cage. I can still easily recall these vivid moments by conjuring up the smells of the watermelon, the mud in the cage, and the smell of Donald himself. I can feel the sticky juice tracks on my arms and hands and feel Donald's bill trying to take some of the seeds from my fingers. And I can't leave out the memory of the blue-colored sky and the sizzling hot sun which was beating down on us. In contrast to the heat, the frosty watermelon became an almost exotic relief and treat. Eventually, this cozy scene turned into my sister Nancy and I bursting into giggles. I'm sure it all started when my brother Jimmy gave one of his famous sideways grins and launched the first of the slippery black seeds at us. The ensuing carefree laughter and screams were surely heard all around the neighborhood as we scampered and jumped to meet the challenge of dodging the seeds. As for Donald, I think he resigned himself to standing stone-cold still while his neck pivoted like a rollercoaster trying to keep up with all the action, hoping some of the succulent seeds would fly his way. That afternoon ended with us all romping in the water of the wildly rotating sprinkler. You might've guessed Mom didn't want us coming in the house looking like we had been tarred and feathered with watermelon juice, seeds, and a few fluffy white feathers attached here and there.

CREATE AN ENCHANTMENT

Think about this memory of mine. Note when each of the five senses were being utilized. What feelings are being conveyed in my telling? What feelings are being evoked? Now find a memory from your own past. Investigate by feeling and sensing it all over again. What makes it special? Connections with others, undivided attention in the moment, creativity? Is it feelings, awareness, newness of an adventure, the intricate environment, laughter, humor, or maybe an open heart? Please allow yourself the pleasure of reminiscing.

Now that your imagination is warmed up, read through the next set of stories engaging even more of your senses and emotions. And for fun and extra credit, play around with experiencing the story from both my point of view as a child and then from my mom's point of view. See what comes up for you!

And don't forget to note that each one of these stories are marvelous recipes for spending fun time with the children in your life.

TREASURES FROM THE SEASONS

Jack Frost

One of my earliest memories as a small child was when Jack Frost would visit our home on cold wintery nights, and we would awaken to the unbelievable intricate designs on our single-paned windows. As we would start to stir on these mornings, Mom, in a slightly whispering voice, would caution us to be a little quiet, as we might be able to catch a glimpse of this artist while he was putting finishing touches on his masterpieces. I can still feel how wonderful it was to be tucked in my cozy warm bed while listening to Mom talking about this elaborately gifted character who seemed to always have time to visit us. Then, as the wood stove would start warming our house, we would watch the delicate artistic strokes slowly turn into robust glistening droplets that played games with each other while they picked up speed as they hastened to the bottom of the window and bounced onto the windowsill.

You might think this was the last of the early morning mysteries, but the next thing that would happen would be Mom holding us up to the windows to see the extra gifts which might have transpired in the world outside. Sometimes, we would find the trees and bushes abundantly piled with frost and intricate patterns of glistening lace. If you looked closely, especially on sunny days, you could see tiny threads of frost with little diamonds strung from branch to branch on bushes and trees. We were always looking for Jack Frost holding his special brush, but we never managed to get up quite early enough to see him. Sometimes we would see a shadow or some movement and think, It might be him! Was it him? We were never sure. We had other questions we would ask Mom from time to time: Did he have helpers? Did he have one brush or many? Did he ever do a pattern more than once? Were his clothes made out of snowflakes so people couldn't see him? Could he vanish into thin air?

As the morning progressed, we would have breakfast and Mom would bundle us up in snow-clothes, and out we would go to frolic and explore the snowy world. Just to paint a really good picture, when I say bundled up, we went out looking like miniature musclemen characters. This was in the days when you needed lots of layers because nothing was waterproof. It was hard to bend over to look at anything, and if you fell over, watch out! You had to trust your playmates to help you up, but nine times out of ten they would be laughing and watching you roll around like a little beached whale.

This getup didn't stop us from investigating the surprises and mysteries that were in store for us on any wintery wonderland day. We proudly created beautiful snow angels which we strategically placed in the fresh expanse of new snow. Other days would find us immersed in wild snowball fights or lively games of Fox and Geese with other kids in the neighborhood. We would build many a snowman and pretend he or she might be dancing around at night, just like Frosty. It was always a task to find objects for the snowmen's faces and their clothing. And Mom would answer the many knocks on the door requesting items like a carrot for the nose or a colorful scarf and some sort of a hat.

But soon we would be tumbling into the house and our wet woolen mittens would start their drying process on the handle of the hot cook stove. It was always interesting that, at first, these wool gloves seemed to smell a little like a wet dog while they steamed their way to dryness.

A Maple Syrup Experience

Inside the house, wintery days unfolded with us taking full advantage of our worlds. Mom would come up with different surprises like having us watch her cook "real" maple syrup, and then she would take the hot pan outside and pour each of us a good helping of the tantalizing amber liquid that magically disappeared into a blanket of freshly fallen snow. After a few long, anticipating moments, Mom would have each of us plunge our hands into the snow to find our sculptured surprise. The syrup had magically turned into a perfect piece of the most delicious candy you could imagine. By the end of enjoying this elegant sugar plum of a treat, our fingers and smiling lips were sublimely sticky. This happened to be part of the fun of this cherished event.

You have to know, one of the things about my mom that made her special was when we were doing a project or creating something, she didn't worry if we or other things were getting a little messy. Her motto was to live and explore to the fullest. She felt it was easy to wash hands, faces, clothes, floors, tables, etc. This freedom to get messy and make a mess was a big gift—we never felt like we were going to get it wrong.

Gingerbread Boys and Girls

Some winter afternoons were for baking. This event literally took on a life of its own. One of our favorite things was to make gingerbread boys and girls. We would start out with Mom helping us to measure out the ingredients. We would manage to dump most of them into the bowl and then we would take turns stirring. It looked a little like a snowstorm had happened inside the house by the time we were ready to make the cookies. Rolling out the dough was done partly by Mom and partly by my sister and me. And we didn't use cookie cutters; we used our own artistic eyes to cut these almost life-sized gingerbread characters into form. Once we had decorated them with raisin eyes and noses, red hot candies for the lips and cheeks, and various vibrant choices for their clothes, it was time to slip them in the old-fashioned oven in our cook stove. Mom would carefully open the impossibly heavy door of the oven and pop these fine specimens of our toil and fun into their final stage of completion. As they cooked, the fragrant ginger and molasses smells enveloped our house creating a mounting culinary anticipation for anyone home at that time.

Mom would coach us on readying ourselves for the

(ENCHANTMENT ALERT!) absolutely real possibility that one or both of our creations might jump up and run out the door when she opened it. She would go to the oven door and very, very slowly open it to give us time to prepare for an ensuing chase around the house or out the door and into the yard. As this drama unfolded, we all three held our breath and were almost perfectly still. To this day, I delight in the memory of the cozy kitchen, our lighthearted laughter, and the magic of possibilities. I have to admit, I always felt a slight hesitation before eating these almost bigger-than-life delicious confections.

Spring Approaches

As spring began to show its tentative footprints in the lingering drifts of snow, a new magic would begin to unfold with the tell-tale signs of a waking world. Mom always honored and marveled at the profound beauty and mystery of spring, and how unbelievable it was that plants, bushes, and trees would start to come back to life after being blanketed in the long visit of winter in our region in Montana.

She instilled in us this admiration, respect, and ability to really watch for the grandeur of the new life that was unfolding. Now, to a child, these events might not have had such deep meaning or captured such intriguing interest without inventive guidance. But, being a creative mom, she came up with a variety of methods for developing in us the kind of attention necessary to cultivate a deep appreciation and respect for our outside environment. Mom definitely had a spring enchantment recipe book!

Enchantment in the Garden

In early spring in the garden, Mom would be down on her hands and knees lifting up fallen leaves and peeking under them to show us the first little sprouts that were poking their heads up. She had us guessing what they were going to become in all their glory as late spring and summer approached. She would also sprinkle a little bit of her fairy and elf wisdom. ENCHANTMENT

ALERT! You could hear her in quiet tones saying things like, "Watch carefully. You might get a glimpse of one of the fairies or elves. They absolutely love spring and the magic of everything waking up." She would encourage us to keep looking around for them. Once spring really arrived, these wee characters would be sure to be popping into flower beds and vegetable gardens everywhere. Of course they would be! There is so much fun and excitement to be had in newly growing things!

Yes, this garden area was included in Mom's recipe. The large yard was her sanctuary, where she would guide us in learning more about the flower garden, the large vegetable garden, and many different fruit trees, plus the other creatures besides the elves and fairies—like spiders! Spiders were, generally, not my favorite; they would scare me almost to death. It seemed they would freely and silently hitch a ride on my arms, in my hair, or on my back. When one of them landed on me, that would get me jumping up and down, screaming, and doing some sort of a wild dance that had the neighbors thinking—well, I'm not sure what they were thinking, but it wasn't good. You see, Mom never sprayed for critters, so we had an abundance of them. There was one type of a little spider I have only seen in Mom's backyard.

They were quite small, and they came with little rounded bellies in light pink and light green shades. She said they were good spiders, and I was sure these adorable puffs of cuteness belonged to the fairy and elf habitat. No, I never tried to pick one up. I actually tried to look them up recently but didn't find the ones I remembered. Maybe I wasn't off-base on their magical connections!

Our Very Own Garden Spaces

My sister and I had our own spaces in my mom's garden area where we spent some time picking out the most colorful and intriguing flowers to entice the fairies and elves. We took delight in the fact that our gardens would be nicely enchanting for the wee characters. The detective work of watching for them to pop in for a visit had us acutely aware of our surroundings.

The Gift of Flowers

It wasn't unusual to see my sister or me with big grins on our faces heading to one of our neighbors' houses with a huge, multicolored bouquet of elegant flowers Mom had picked in her garden. I can remember not being able to see over the tops of some of them. I think we felt like we were the fairy and elf helpers because the flowers came from our own fascinating, magical garden. I don't really think that I ever understood until I was much older how much being the recipient of these vibrant, intricate bouquets must have meant to our neighbors. We had a number of older neighbors who didn't get out much. Mom always had a giving heart.

Hunting for Four-Leaf Clovers

ENCHANTMENT ALERT! I can still hear my Mom saying in an almost mysterious voice, "Look, it's a beautiful patch of clover! You know what might be hidden in here by one of the leprechauns or elves?" We would bounce up and down and answer in excited tones that one of us might find A FOUR-LEAF CLOVER! And we knew it would bring us good luck, or, at least, let us know one of the wee characters might be hiding behind some flowers or up in a tree to watch as we employed our great explorer talents. My mom patiently passed on her expert ways of inspecting each and every clover leaf for that extra bit of summer magic. Kneeling or lying on our stomachs while systematically searching for the desired valuable treasures from nature found us intrigued for some time. My mom was an expert in finding clover patches. After she was no longer with us, I was going through her purse and found, carefully placed between the plastic sheets in her wallet, a faded four-leaf clover. Did she feel it would bring her the magic of good luck, or did she keep it to remember the lazy time on a summer's day spent making magic with her children and grandchildren?

I still find myself drawn to stooping down and taking a quick look for one of those rare twists of nature. You might ask about how many four-leaf bits of wonder I've found in my life. I have found just three or four of them. Just enough to keep me interested in the journey of exploration, which continues to this day. Recently, on a trip to the Oregon coast with my husband, we found several abundant patches of rather large clover which had me again peering along the pathways for one of these rare presents from nature—or perhaps from a wee character.

Mud Pies Anyone?

Here you will find a totally free, hours-of-fun activity that everyone can easily try: mud pies. It was one of Mom's favorites for interacting with the realness of our environments. You need soil, the kind you find in the garden or by a creek; a decent supply of water from a hose or small stream; your hands; and a good dose of your creative abilities. Add in any tools you'd like to help with your creations: trays, little dishes, silverware, sticks, sand, and/or rocks. With these supplies, you will find yourselves fully engaged in this project of creating the most exceptional mud pies, cakes, characters, etc. By the end, you will be looking for the final touches by using grasses, leaves, and berries to enrich your projects. Mom would even let us use some flowers from the garden to support our works of art that we would oftentimes gift to the elves and fairies. In writing this, I can easily conjure up the happiness in our complete absorption in these projects and the happiness and satisfaction in what we could fashion.

I would encourage you to try this, at least once, while introducing a child into this robust combination of nature meeting youthful spunk. Notice the smell of the soil, the feel of it on your hands, and all the fresh smells and sights around you. Plus, don't forget to note the intensity of creativity streaming from you and your companions.

And let's not forget the cleanup! This sets up a whole separate section of fun: the hose, a sprinkler, or stream usually becomes the main source in helping with cleanup of little hands, faces, and clothes. I will leave that part up to your imaginations for the kind of hilarity that's possible. Just remember to preserve the creations.

To the Mountains with Great Anticipation of Adventures

Now this is where Mom may have come up with additional parts to her recipe to fully capture our imaginations. On top of a high mountain, where things were dry, and the sun felt like it was going to fry you like an egg, is where you might find the much sought-after sparkling gems that are crystals! ENCHANTMENT ALERT! The shiny, beautifully-shaped prizes from the hot, dry dirt had to be gifts from the wee ones—or did they just love being around them? I think this even had my mom intrigued. When she would pull a faceted, chiseled crystal out of the ground, she would often look at it and then peer around, thinking she might get a chance to see one of those wee characters clicking their feet in midair, while twirling around in delight. Mom seemed to always know she would come across them. One of Mom's thoughts was the elves and fairies might have planted the crystals in these areas. Maybe they wanted to make them playfully sparkle in the sun to intrigue people dedicated enough to sit on

a mountaintop carefully digging for them in the intense sun of a summer's day. Either way, Mom was an expert when it came to finding many shapes and sizes of these radiant rainbow catchers. The thought of finding them had us captivated and investigating very closely. We would dig for the crystals, but I must say, we did a lot more running around looking for proof of the elves and fairies.

Picnic Adventures with Mom and Dad,
and the Lure of the Wee Folk

ENCHANTMENT ALERT! When we went to the mountains with Mom and Dad for picnics, the doors to the car would fly open as we enthusiastically tumbled out of the car with agility and curiosity. The woods seemed to welcome us with the sounds of the squirrels chattering and the birds chirping and singing while comically flitting around. With this trumpeting serenade, we were sure the fairies and elves were well aware of our excited entrance into their worlds. That was good, but it didn't leave much of a chance that we would be able to surprise them and get a glance of these whimsical characters before they disappeared.

But it was really okay. We figured if they knew we had arrived, it gave them just enough time to hastily leave us strategically placed clues.

These clues always made us feel confident they were close by: mushrooms in different sizes and shapes, wildflowers, and little pools of water that were just plain magical. From time to time, we would be able to catch one of their amphibious pets, a real live slippery frog or a weird-looking toad.

The elves and fairies also shared their different berry patches: raspberries, blackberries and strawberries. They looked just like the ones we had at home, but their tastes were somehow deliciously enhanced. We felt they were probably touched by fairy dust.

Huckleberry Patches: The Unspoken Protocol and Protections

It's especially important to mention that the other berry in this domain is the huckleberry! We learned from a young age that spotting one of these huckleberry patches is exceedingly rare and therefore it is best to keep quiet about it. If someone overhears you mentioning you were huckleberry picking, the first question out of their sly smiling mouths might be, "And where did you say the huckleberry patch is located?" One of the things as a small child living in Montana you quickly learn is the location of huckleberry patches are well-guarded secrets, and this spoken and unspoken message continues to be true today. It is always a big surprise when you get to "your" patch in the mountains and someone else is there picking, or they drive up and get out of their car and start picking in what you consider "YOUR" patch, and you find out they consider it "THEIR" patch.

Just imagine this scene! The lazy afternoon of picking berries turns into a fast-forwarded movie with fingers moving faster than the eye can see while both self-proclaimed owners look up at each other with guarded, congenial smiles. They might exchange a couple of pleasantries, but their fingers never stop the frenzied pace of harvesting the luscious berries. Now the taste of the huckleberry is a little hard to describe. If you mix a few sun-ripened wild strawberries and raspberries together and add a dose of a summer peach, you might be getting close.

So, you can see when the fairies and elves let you find their huckleberry patches, it is a true gift. To this day I still like to leave a few perfect berries here and there, just in case.

A quick warning if you own a dog and plan on bringing it to the mountains when you go huckleberry picking: the dog will be picking right along with you. At least, our two dogs—little Lhasa Apso pooches—did just that. At first, they were eating one berry at a time, which we thought was so cute! But we became a little concerned when they started to close their front teeth onto the branches of berries, and while keeping their mouths closed, they would pull against the bush and almost smile, as they had the little berries bursting flavor into their mouths. That turned them into competition!

Senses Activated!

So, as we wipe our mouths clean of the delicious huckleberry juice, take a moment to note your experience as you read the stories of how my mother brought us into the world of imagination and play. Could you feel the sunshine on your face, the sticky berry juice on your hands, the delight of searching for crystals or huckleberries? Note the feelings which came along with these sensations. Of course, all this is now in your imagination. It is second-hand because you heard a story from someone else. Think of how much more encompassing these kinds of experiences are when you are living them in the moment. Think of how much it means to the children in our lives to be a part of these experiences. And what is it that makes these times so special? Is it the experience itself or the quality in the time with someone else? Or is it both?

CHAPTER 3

CREATIVITY PERSONALIZED

Each child is unique, and your interaction with each child will be as unique as the child and as unique as you are. Here are some examples with different children and how I played in the field of imagination with each one. Feel free to use these ideas and adapt them to create beautiful creative playgrounds with the children in your life.

SUZANNE'S ELF

My first experiment introducing creativity into a child's magical thinking stage was with my marvelous, unsuspecting niece Suzanne, my sister's daughter. I was fortunate enough to have spent a lot of time with her in her early years. Creative playfulness came naturally to both of us, and we really had fun together!

Introducing Fred, Suzanne's Elf

ENCHANTMENT ALERT! Suzanne and I had a lot of fun with one of the wee folk. The first time Fred the elf showed up was with a little note and a small, wrapped present. It was left on my windowsill when Suzanne was visiting. In the note, Fred introduced himself and let Suzanne know he had decided to be her new friend and would be showing up from time to time. From here, we talked about how Fred might be around and how he would disappear as soon as we looked his way. If we heard a new noise, or we would find a special rock or object on a pathway, we would consider the likelihood of him being close by. We would speculate if some of his friends like the fairies and other elves might come visiting. These moments could just pop into our awareness any time. Suzanne sweetly knew he thought that she was spectacularly fascinating. He continued to bring her gifts and notes. A gift might be as small as a chocolate coin covered in gold, a little colorful rock, or a flower. We knew he loved being around to join in any looming adventures we might cook up. We would laugh and talk about him being involved in our thrilling moments of intrigue.

The Chomping Jaws

I remember, on several occasions, we would pretend an alligator would be chasing us, and we would be screaming and jumping on beds, chairs, and couches to escape its large, rhythmically chomping jaws of terror. Fleeing for our lives, we would run across the floor or out the front door onto the large expanse of grass. To this day, the excitement and drama of these enthralling adventures remain vivid in my memories. I do contemplate, at times, if the alligator remembers these adventures as fondly as I do, or if he is still wishing he had caught at least one of us?

SPENCER'S FRIENDS

My first child, Spencer, came equipped in this world with a great ability to jump into life while utilizing a great imagination. Living with him was a delight. He never missed an opportunity to wander around the world of possibilities.

Interacting with Books Coming to Life

One of the early things we did together was reading, but we would go beyond just reading the books by adding our own twists to the stories. With a little encouragement, Spencer would dive deep into what books had to offer—other than what meets the eye. (If you have never tried this with a young child, please go ahead and give it a whirl. It will bring smiles to your face and warmth to your heart once you do.) Almost any children's picture book would do. We would start reading, and I would see something of interest like an apple, a yummy confection, or a bottle of something to drink. Then I would say something like, "How would you like to taste this or that?" And then I would pretend to pluck it out of the book, and we would both enjoy it to its fullest, sometimes ending up licking our fingers if it was extra delicious. We could talk about its taste or how it felt in our hands. We were more than willing to share one with someone else if they were in the room. Spencer would jump down from the couch or chair and run bearing the luscious gift to them. Surprisingly, there was always enough to go around. Spencer would often wait until they had finished this treat to see what they thought of it or if they wanted another. If they did request a second helping, he would run back to the book and pluck out another prize for the receptive guest. This was a favorite part of our reading and interacting with books.

Another example is if there was something like a cute fluffy animal in a picture, we could pop it out of the pages and pet it. We would talk about how the fur felt, laugh if it jumped up and kissed our noses, and let it snuggle in for a brief minute before we popped it back into the safety of its home in the pages. We knew its mom and dad would be worried if we kept it out too long. When we were cuddled up reading books, there were worlds of senses and sensations to be explored.

The Little White Mouse and Day Care

ENCHANTMENT ALERT! I remember one time, when Spencer was two years old just before he headed to day care, I put a little white mouse in his hands. He tucked it into his pocket and off he went. I didn't think much more about that sweet interaction until one day the owner of the day care said she needed to talk with me about Spencer.

We went into another room and with an uncomfortable look, she said she didn't know how to tell me this, but Spencer had been taking this white mouse out of his pocket and he was showing the other kids! She waited for me to respond, but I waited. She said, "The thing is, he doesn't have a mouse!" I looked at her in amazement. I concluded she, as a day care owner, wasn't familiar with the magical thinking stage in children. I simply said, "He has a great imagination. He takes the mouse everywhere."

I'm not sure if she ever looked at the two of us the same after this private session. Not surprisingly, we ended up at that day care for only twelve weeks total.

The Joy in Disguises

When Spencer was a bit older, starting at about three, on any given day, you could find the two of us on some sort of adventure. He tried on many disguises. Some of his favorites were: a detective, a muscle man, a chef, and a cowboy.

The Detective

He had a great outfit for the detective transformation: a mustache that I would glue on him, a real detective's hat, and a detective's coat. (I had found a tweed men's jacket at the Goodwill shop and altered it down to his size.) He filled the jacket pockets with a small note pad and pencil, a tiny toy revolver, and a magnifying glass. We went down many a street and alley finding clues and treasures: bottle caps, a coin here or there, rocks, or some little broken toy.

The Muscle Man

The muscle man didn't come often, but when he was around, Spencer found his large muscle arms helpful if he needed extra strength. It was a bit of a surprise if all of a sudden, when he was wrestling someone like his dad, there would be a sudden loud pop and one of his muscles would disappear. (I guess balloons aren't always what they are cracked up to be.) To this day he is still lifting weights and staying in great shape.

The Chef

Oh, did I mention he was an engaged cook? He was great with food both imaginary and real. His cooking career started at a young age. I taught him to crack eggs when he turned three, and within a couple of sessions, he was quite proficient. From this age and onward, you could find him in the kitchen experimenting. As he stood on the countertop to reach the spices, or on a ladder to reach the countertops, he would pick out different spices by their smell and remembered tastes. He would add them to his creative concoction in the bowl. Generally, he would also add an egg, a little flour, and a rising agent. The first couple of years I did some teaching on the wisdom of how ingredients work together. I didn't at all mind him using different kitchen supplies for his experiments. By five years old, he was getting pretty good at his skills. With supervision, he could crack and scramble his own eggs. In his mind, a real, professional chef couldn't compete with his inventions. One time, when he was about ten years old, he met us at the door with a satisfied grin on a lightly floured face and body, and said, "Guess what I made?" We walked into a room with the drama of white dust still trying to settle and found a pan of beautifully-shaped homemade pretzels. He said he looked the recipe up by himself and did it all. They were excellent! His love of creative cooking is still an important part of his life.

The Cowboy

As for being a cowboy, Spencer played this part well. Most of the days when he went to preschool, he went as a cowboy. He had a beautiful felt cowboy hat; several different scarves to tie around his neck, an ornate set of chaps and spurs, and two leather vests lined with sheep skin. This was another time we were pulled in to visit with the teacher. This time, the teacher looked a bit apologetic, and delicately let us know Spencer was turning everything he played with into a gun. Well, thinking we had been being conscientious parents, we had made the choice to not get him toy guns. But this meeting had us running out to find a couple of six shooters and a holster to complete his outfit. Problem settled; he wasn't able to take them to school, which was fine with him. At this same meeting, she let us know Spencer was the only one that came to school dressed up as different characters. You see, he made use of all of his disguises when he went to preschool, but being the cowboy was his favorite. The teacher said she loved having his inventive spirit in her classroom. Since he was our first child, we didn't realize this wasn't the norm. I would have him do it all over, again, if it was his desire. I treasure those days and memories.

Spencer's Elves: Huberty-Duber

I'm not sure where to begin explaining about this impressive creation of a new personality in our lives. I think Spencer was close to three years old when the first elf, Huberty-Duber, presented himself. Spencer turned into this elf whenever he desired to pop into our world. There were no disguises for this charming character. I would know when Huberty-Duber came to visit; he had his own way of talking, different facial expressions, and he was a little light-footed, as if he was going to jump a foot into the air at any moment. He didn't mind at all if I saw him. He might show up for a few minutes or for the whole afternoon. One day he told me to watch him jump off the barbecue. I stood at the kitchen window and watched as he scampered out the back door to the tall brick barbecue. With a little effort, he climbed up the side where I thought he was going to jump from, but no, he then scampered up the chimney and literally seemed to fly off the back of it to the ground. It was a six-foot drop to the grass below. I stood stark still for a second, and then I went running out the back door thinking I would find him crumpled on the other side with maybe two broken legs or worse. As I reached him, he was getting up and broadly smiled, and quite proudly asked, "Do you want me to do that, again?!" Well, that made me let Huberty-Duber know this wasn't something he could do again, and I would also let Spencer know about this limit. He understood.

(More of) Spencer's Elves: Luberty-Duber

A couple of months later, another elf started to visit, and this time Luberty-Duber was his name. Again, it didn't take long to recognize him. He started sharing the time he came to visit with Huberty-Duber. Over the years, they ended up being the two main elves. I spent many an adventure with them. I remember one early evening when Spencer, three years old, came to visit me at the hospital where I worked, and we had dinner in the cafeteria. As we were getting up to leave, a kindly lady at the table next to us motioned for us to come over. She smiled and looked up at me with misty eyes, "I have to tell you how much it has meant for me to sit next to you with your imaginative child. My grandson had the same type of imagination, and I loved it so much. I truly cherish all of those memories with him! They were so exceptionally precious!" I introduced her to Luberty-Duber, he gave her an elf smile, shook her hand, and away we disappeared into the crowd.

Spencer's Elves: Best Friends, Biff and Selly

You might be pondering who popped up next. Well, it wasn't one elf, but two of them. And why two of them at once? I will explain the friendship between Biff and Selly. It seemed Biff would come first. Biff was non-speaking. He would try to pantomime what he wanted us to understand. He was very patient and creative in trying to get me or someone else to try to guess what he was trying to express. A good game of Charades couldn't compare with the inventive, rich expressions from Biff. Unfortunately, we couldn't always guess what he was trying to portray. At these times, he would wander off to elf land which might be hidden in another room, behind a couch, or down the stairs.

You guessed it, then Selly would pop into our lives. Selly was the best of friends with Biff. He would always let us know what Biff had wanted us to understand. They started coming to visit when Spencer was close to four years old.

Several months after our well-loved addition of Biff and Selly, with their wisdom and patience, plus their creativity, we were blessed with another bit of charm. This little elf, and I mean little, was a baby elf named Hamburger-Raisin. He basically crawled right into our lives.

We usually saw him at dinner, most of the time. There is a bit of important information to help you understand the need for his entrance. You see, Spencer did not like broccoli. Try as he might, it wasn't his favorite. At these times, Spencer would say it was time for him to go to elf and fairy land, and he would be excused from the table. In minutes, we would find Hamburger-Raisin crawling to us from his enchanted land. We would pick him up and put him in Spencer's chair and invite him to eat with us. We would talk to him, and pat his little head, but the conversations were limited; he was so sweetly still a baby elf. But one word he could almost pronounce was "baaklee." This young elf loved broccoli! You could hear him saying, much of the time, "more baaklee." After wholeheartedly enjoying every bite, it was time for him to go.

He would try crawling down, with help from me, and would head back to elf and fairy land. I would be saying and waving goodbye, and reminding him to send Spencer home, if he saw him. Very shortly Spencer would come around the corner and tell us all sorts of tales that happened on his visit.

The Big Shaggy Dog from Elf and Fairy Land

One of the other delightful creatures was the big furry dog from the world of the elves and fairies. He would come bounding into the house with his long hair flowing from side to side. He would flop his head on your knees and want pets, scratches behind his ears, and to get his hair ruffled. If you were on the floor with him, he might give you big slobbery kisses. I loved this wild, frolicking creature.

The Leprechaun

Last but not least, a leprechaun that came to visit. He was quite charming, and interestingly enough, easy to spot: he had a green hat and a little multi-colored striped scarf he always wore when he visited. He didn't have a name, just an abundant propensity for climbing on things and jumping off. He always had a twinkle in his eyes and a mischievous way about himself.

A Curious Visit to the Doctor

One family member who had Spencer's best interests at heart was very concerned he was forming multiple personalities. When she would call and someone like Huberty-Duber would answer, she would say, "Now, who is this?" And when Huberty-Duber would identify himself, she would say, "Spencer, I know that is you!"

At the end of one of his doctor's appointments, I let the doctor know of her concerns. The doctor said, "Well, can I meet one of these personalities?"

To which I replied, "Well, you have been talking to Luberty-Duber this whole time."

The doctor shook hands with Luberty-Duber and proceeded to chat with him for a moment. Then he said to Luberty-Duber, "Can I say hi to Spencer?"

With a smile and a nod, Luberty-Duber popped down from the exam table and went behind it. It looked like he was walking down a staircase until he was completely gone. And in another second, out came Spencer from around the exam table.

The doctor put out his hand and shook Spencer's hand, and said, "And who am I talking to now?"

Spencer raised an eyebrow, and looked at him with some disbelief, which I believe he was thinking "How could his doctor not recognize me? He has known me for years."

Spencer looked him square in the eyes and said, "I'm Spencer!"

The doctor looked at me with a genuine smile and said, "Just go home and totally enjoy your creative child."

We did let everyone who was concerned know that Spencer wasn't going to slip into adult life with any issues with multiple personalities with his five different elves, a big shaggy dog, or as a bouncy leprechaun. All were simply a child's rich imagination at work.

I can't say exactly when these well-loved characters started staying more and more in elf and fairy land. I remember that Spencer was six years old when they last visited. As the lady in the cafeteria smilingly told me, enjoy every moment, and I did!

ERIKA'S PRAYERS

The Sandman

Talk about someone who could escape going to bed on time. That was Erika, my daughter who was six years younger than Spencer, her brother. Starting at about two, it was clear that she believed there were always more options in life than meets the eye. Or there's more than one way to skin a cat, as they say. Who would ever think the Sandman would be my trump card? It would go a little like this: I would warn her, "Erika, I just heard something at the door," or "I saw movement outside the window! I think the Sandman is close by. Hurry!" It would reduce her stalling, directing her creative spirit to a blur of movement as she popped into bed. We would have enough time to say prayers and then talk about what crystals of radiant colors she wanted the Sandman to leave in the corners of her eyes to help her with requested dreams for the night. "What color of sparkles do you want tonight? What dreams do you want tonight?" I would ask. After a minute or two, I would, again, let her know I heard something and whisper, "I think I hear him! Shhhh." And I would quietly disappear out her bedroom door after giving her a hug and a kiss.

ENCHANTMENT ALERT! It was well known if you weren't in bed and, at least, almost asleep, the Sandman would probably pass you by. Then you would end up with regular sand in the corner of your eyes, rather than the rainbow of colors you picked the night before to help you have your chosen dreams. Now, who wants that? Yes, in the morning, the sand looks the same, but it did sparkle all night with the promise of influencing the youthful requests for a night of whimsical imaginings.

Prayers Before Bed

With Erika I would say prayers before bed. She actually repeated what I would say, prayers for other people or situations in the world to something she might need help with. At the end of the prayer, I would ask her, "What made you happy today? What did you like best about yourself, today? What do you want to tell God?"—or whatever seemed to fit for the day. At one point, when she was eleven, she stopped repeating what I was saying, and I asked her why. She said, "Mom, I'm not repeating the dumb stuff, anymore." I figured she was more than ready to say them by herself. At this point, with love and a bit of sadness, I realized it was one of the letting go times of sweet, special sharing.

A Prayer Answered with a Watering Can

This is one of my favorite stories about Erika's prayers. Erika was six years old. We were on a whirlwind of adventure as we traveled from one garage sale to another while shopping for treasures. She wanted a watering can for her little flower bed. We had been out for about two hours and needed to rush home to get ready for an afternoon wedding. I said if we find one more garage sale on our way home, we will have just enough time to stop. She said a little prayer asking God to help her find a watering can. Well, we made one very quick stop.

Two older women were sitting behind their little table enjoying the wealth of friendship on a sunny day. They both smiled and happily greeted us. We were only there a couple of minutes, and Erika looked quickly for the watering can which did not appear. We thanked them as we hurried on our way. One of the women, called after us, "Was there something special you were looking for?" Erika said, "I wanted a watering can for my flowers." The lady said, "Sorry, I don't have one." As we were getting in the car, she motioned us back. She said with a smile, "You know, I do have a watering can in my garage. I will get. I got it years ago. My husband wasn't totally in favor of it; he didn't think I would use it. Well, he was right. I used it for a short while and now it sits in my garage." She asked Erika how much she would like to spend on it, and Erika showed her dollar. She said, "You just enjoy this." Well, that watering can sat on our front porch for years, reminding us Erika's prayer was pleasantly answered.

MADI'S ADVENTURES

Madi and Grandma's Secret Recipe!

Spencer's daughter Madi and I have such fun together! Our recipe: throw in our five senses at heightened levels. Add several doses of playful imagination, and shake it all in a creative space filled with marvelous sounds, light and dark shading, surprises, and many textures. Next: add energy and enchantment. Add the secret ingredient of curiosity via the amused child and adult, and let the adventures begin. Actually, add as many children and adults as you would like, and then the liveliness and memories explode into an array of delight and giggles. Being a part of this club means you must come open to discovery, laughter, and adventure.

Grandma and Madi Jitterbugging

With agile, insistent, carefree rhythms, Madi and I were transported into energetic movement that had us jitterbugging back and forth across the gleaming white bathroom tiles. When the music stopped, we found ourselves in fits of giggles and promised each other this—our spontaneous choreography— would be our secret, which we kept for years. Recently, we did divulge our secret of pleasant silliness to a wider circle, and now to all of you. That hasn't stopped us from finding ourselves tapping and moving our feet to captivating country music when the setting is to our liking. Our criteria: the space needs to be large enough and we don't spy any feet under the stalls. This secret tradition started when we happened to be dining in a very nice restaurant. We excused ourselves to go to the ladies' room, and it just happened we were alone in this very spacious and charming bathroom when the cowboy jitterbug music burst into our space. Madi was seven years old, and judging by this demonstration of youthfulness, I must have been rather young myself, or maybe just old enough to take advantage of a perfect opportunity. We are both still up for the merriment that can find us dancing into this bit of fancy.

Mitzi's Trip Around the World

Speaking of an adventure that started from an accident, Mitzi, Madi's fairy, broke her porcelain leg. It plain shattered when she flew backwards off the cutout wall behind the couch. This all happened when Madi invited Mitzi to Christmas morning to watch us all open presents. She sat her down in a place where I thought she might not be safe. Well, Grandma (that would be me) picked her up and put her on the ledge of the cutout which would be away from everyone. My granddaughter said, "Grandma, she will fall off!" As I turned to reassure her Mitzi was very safe, I saw the look of terror in my son Spencer's eyes as he leapt up to try to grab Mitzi as she flew to the lower level and onto the hard stairs far, far below.

This memory is clearly etched in my mind! I can still see it all happening from Spencer and Madi bringing Mitzi upstairs while I was standing totally still thinking this has to be a dream. There were tears in all of our eyes. Spencer retrieved some purple dressing tape and wrapped the remainder of the fairy's shattered leg. Jenny, Madi's mom, sadly picked up the remaining pieces of Mitzi's leg off the stairs and put them carefully into a small box. And this was the beginning of that Christmas morning.

But, as my mother would say, "Generally, there is something good that comes from most things." At that time, the only thing I could think of was nothing else was broken except our hearts.

The something good: Over the next several weeks, when I would talk with Madi, she would reassure me she was sure Mitzi's leg was growing back by little millimeters.

ENCHANTMENT ALERT! Then, out of the clear blue, Mitzi went on a trip to different Fairy Festivals around the world. She left Madi a note before she departed, letting Madi know she would return. During those several months when she was gone, she would send Madi presents and notes from different parts of the world letting her know she was having so much fun with all of the new sights, sounds, and experiences. She always reassured Madi she missed her and she would soon return. We were all relieved, ecstatic, in fact, when Mitzi returned with her leg perfectly healed!

Fairies and elves love exploring, traveling, and learning about new and different ideas and interests. You may not have realized it, but they totally enjoy going to museums, art houses, gardens, fairs, and they particularly love going to zoos. They have a real love of what life has to offer and can actually show up about anywhere.

JESSIE BEAN'S VISIONS

Fairies and Elves at the Summer Fair

ENCHANTMENT ALERT! Running at lighting speed, dodging in and out of people, Jessie Bean, my granddaughter, called behind her as she raced to a majestic old pine tree, "Grandma, there's a fairy and elf door in this tree!" It only took seconds to find myself kneeling next to her at the bottom of this stately giant. This wise four-year-old whispered, "I know this is a doorway, and it didn't disappear. I know elves or fairies live here! Look up, Grandma, there are some holes for windows up there! I just

saw a squirrel peeking at us. He is a friend of the fairies, you know." This was the start of our adventure in this awe-inspiring old park where many gifted artists were selling their works at the Sweet Pea Festival. Jessie and I were left alone on this captivating adventure, while her mom Jenny and sister Madi went in a different direction. With all the talented exhibiters there, I must tell you, the fairies and elves weren't a part of what I was thinking this day would be about, initially. My initial thoughts of strolling through the vendors' elaborate booths filled with their creations disappeared. They were replaced by the intriguing richness of walking into the wee people's world with my guide, Jessie Bean, directing each and every discovery while others unknowingly passed by. Jessie Bean ran, skipped, and carefully inspected many different spots of the wee people's hidden worlds: doorways in carved-out rocks, mossy areas, mushrooms, water features, and many sounds that would support their existence. At one point, under the corner of one of the artists' tables, she found a little house that was built out of sticks, pine cones, leaves, and moss. It was actually carefully constructed by some little fingers with just the right touch of knowing what a fellow investigator would recognize. The lady at the table said she didn't know anything about it. Until that day, I really didn't have a clear idea of how much Jessie Bean knew about the lore of these wee characters and their habitats until she compellingly led me around the large park pointing out all of the elusive, fascinating clues of their existence. I will always cherish this day and the treasures we shared in this wonderland.

Adventures on a Hike: the Huckleberry Tradition Continues!

I was just beginning to wake from the night's slumber when, out of the corner of my eye, I thought I heard and saw something! An elf, a fairy, no, it was Jessie Bean, then nine years old, standing beside my bed peering intently at me. She whispered, when she saw my eyes starting to open, "Grandma, are you awake? When are we leaving to the mountains to take a hike and pick huckleberries?" Well, the morning officially started. Grandpa was in the kitchen making his coffee, up and ready for the day. Jessie Bean jumped in bed with me for a few snuggles and whispers before we bounded out of our cozy nest, dressed, and ate breakfast. We were in the car even before Grandpa. You see, two weeks earlier, Jessie Bean's sister Madi was with Grandpa and me when we found a huckleberry patch, but most of the berries weren't quite ripe. This bit of information set the stage of anticipation for this day of exploring and gathering. "Is it around this bend, Grandpa, how about around the next one? Are there fairies and elves that live here? I saw a pine cone being thrown to the ground! And over there is a whole field of wildflowers." Jessie mused and observed all the while as she picked up speed to inspect this field of radiance. She is a strong hiker and never complains; half the time she is bounding around like a yearling while investigating the bountiful gifts of the forest.

Grandpa finally announced, "This is it." Well, it was it! The slope was still as steep as I had remembered. We looked around to find the best footing for getting up this formidable mountainside. The lure of the huckleberries had us taking chances that might have been questionable. Jessie Bean and I were sticking close by each other on the steeper parts; I tightly hung onto her when we moved from location to location when the impending doom of the cliffs were looming only a few feet away. A few times we just sat down and flat out laughed. I'm not sure if it was out of merriment, exhaustion, just plain fear, or a combination of all of it. The unspoken agreement of huckleberry pickers is nothing will stop them from getting their succulent berries. Well, I must add, the only exception, spoken or unspoken, is when you hear someone scream "Bear!" and you see something that resembles a bear. Until this moment, I never thought of a fellow huckleberry picker dressing up like a bear to secure the patch for themselves....hummm. That's an idea. For those of you that aren't aware of the preciousness of these berries in Montana, they are selling anywhere from $50 to $80 per gallon. "Grandma, do you think we have enough to make jam?" Jessie Bean kept asking. About two hours into this intense operation, we decided to head back to our car.

Jessie protectively put herself in charge of carrying the berries housed in a clear plastic bag to the car. She was the first to spot a family of four coming up the trail, and she greeted them with a pleasant, but guarded smile, and a rather quick, "Hi" as she intently continued hiking at what seemed a steady, fast clip.

As she turned and looked up the trail, she could see Grandpa was a short ways behind us, and he had stopped to talk to the family. She looked at me with concerned, wide eyes, and in a whisper, questioned, "What if Grandpa tells them what we were hunting, and where? I put the huckleberries behind my back so they wouldn't see them, and I'm sure they didn't!" I reassured her Grandpa would have "zipped his lips" if they questioned him about our secret.

"Do we have everything we need for the jam? Will we do it today? I have the energy!" she assured us with a big smile. "Mom and Dad are going to be so excited! And I can't wait to learn how to make jam!"

Four miles back to the car and another hour and a half to drive home found the three of us putting our day's pickings in the fridge. Then, after using the last of our energy to make popcorn, we headed upstairs, cuddling up to watch a movie, and a retelling of our adventures from the successful huckleberry gathering day.

Scrumptious Berry Jars of Summer Memories

Let's get back to the jam. The next day we ended up adding raspberries from my niece's garden, the huckleberries, and some chokecherries from the trees in the yard. Jessie Bean washed berries, measured out ingredients, and stirred until everything turned into the sweetest-smelling, most stunning ruby red pot of bubbling enchantment either of us had ever seen! She definitely had another significant notch in her culinary belt. We carefully labeled the jars with her name proudly displayed. Her family members were the recipients of a number of precious jars of her toil and adventures.

Bedtime Bunny Stories

It is tradition that I tell Jessie Bean a bedtime story when I'm with her. I tell her silly little stories about two bunnies that bounce and hop around on her and in her bed. When they tire, I tuck them around her neck or under her arms, and they all three pleasantly fall into the coziness of imaginary friendship. We both love this tradition. Depending on the night, it might only take two or three minutes, but it is our time.

GREYSON'S MAGICAL THINKING

Greyson, my daughter's son, is six years old at the writing of this book. He is naturally full of enthusiasm and, oftentimes, he uses words and thoughts that seem above his pay grade of experience. The memories I relate to you about him in this book are amusingly accurate.

The Seemingly Live Elf

At age four, Greyson was in the store with his Grandma Loni (his dad's mom) and kept pulling on her hand. She finally asked him what he was doing, and he whispered, "There is a real live elf over there." And he was looking straight into the eyes of an elf or little girl his size. He wanted his grandmother to be very quiet so she, the possible elf, didn't disappear.

44

Greyson Testing Reality

More recently, at age four-almost-five, I was on the phone with him, and he surmises, "Grandma, there is something really suspicious going on. Do you bring the elf and fairy presents in your purse? They always come when you are here." I could honestly say I didn't bring them in my purse. You might be questioning if he actually said, "suspicious," and he did. Not once, but several appropriately placed times in this exploration.

Fast forward to when he is five and a visit to our house for his first overnight stay without his mom and dad, he asked, "Grandma, are you awake? I'm going to look for the elf and fairy presents. They always come when we are together." And tradition continues.

A Sweet Nighttime Tradition

Age five, just barely, Greyson declared, "I'm really scared if we sleep with the lights off. Will you hold my hand? I know I am working on my fear. I don't want to grow up and be afraid of the dark!" So, with him in a cot next to my bed, we held hands until he fell asleep. This is a very special memory. The simple pleasure of holding his little, trusting hand in mine for many minutes had my heart glowing. We now repeat this tradition whenever I have the delightful opportunity of spending the night with him.

When Will the Calves Be Born?

Another time, while dealing with an exceptionally determined five-year-old Greyson, his dad Lance looked at me with a little sign of frustration, and said, "Greyson doesn't want to go with you and Mary today. He wants to stay home." (Mary is my good friend.) Greyson was standing with his little arms wrapped tightly around his body, his jaw set, with a look of sadness and firmness that would have stopped most grandparents in their tracks.

I pushed forward, "Greyson, if you want to stay home, maybe we could go out to lunch with Mary first, and then I can bring you back here. We were planning on going to the museum after lunch, or anything else you might like to do."

Like any good rancher—like his dad—he states, "I can't leave because my cows are going to calve this afternoon and I need to be here to help them!" It really seemed to be the end of the story. The sense of responsibility weighed heavy with his duty to care for his cattle.

A little frustrated, Lance said, "Your cows will wait until you come home. It is time to go with Grandma."

Greyson strongly refuted this idea, and explained they were his cows, saying "I know it's this afternoon, and I can't leave them."

I said, "Usually they calve at night, I bet they will wait for you. We might go to the climbing wall?"

His face started to soften, a bit, and he said, "I want to go to the climbing wall, but then I will need to come right home."

When we picked Mary up, he told her of his frustrations. She repeated that the cows would probably calve at night. He said, "How do you know?" She straightforwardly said, "They are your toy cows, they will wait for you, because you are their owner." This seemed to quiet his strong feelings of responsibility while abandoning his livestock in their possible hours of need.

And off we went for a full day of adventures. This included: lunch, a trip to the museum which was equipped with life-sized dinosaurs and Greyson's favorite, a fishing pond in the children's section, and a nap at Mary's house to revitalize his energy. Then a visit to his cousin's house for an afternoon of carefree youthful play, plus swimming and splashing in the hot tub with the girls, Madi and Jessie. The climbing wall didn't work out; his permission slip wasn't current. Until the next time.

When we arrived home, he raced to his bedroom! He was relieved to find none of his cows had calved after all. This is a wonderful example of the magical thinking stage of a five-year-old! You have to respect the realness of their sincerity as their worlds unfold. In the magical thinking stage, the worlds of the child's imagination are as real to them as the real world is to you and me. We grownups can help our little ones by respecting the rich worlds they create around themselves. And when we give that gift to them, we get the gift of being transported into their grand imaginings.

Bonus: Olivia and the Whimsical Horse

One day, Olivia, my granddaughter, innocently questioned me, "Grandma, do you think the horse jumped out of the painting last night, and ran around the house? How does he get back in the picture?" You see, we have a painting of a rather whimsical horse that emits enough personality to be intriguing to a curious six-year-old. From time to time, we would pretend we were jumping into the picture to pet the horse. I had let her know it would be interesting if he jumped out of the painting and ran around the house just for the fun of it while we were sleeping. We giggled while we talked about it kicking up its heels and running around in enthusiastic freedom. I still look at the picture and think of those captured moments of sharing and smile at the thought of this whimsical character prancing about our home undetected.

Easter Morning

Greyson, now six years old, called me bright and early. He burst out, "The Easter Bunny came last night and guess what he brought me? A chocolate squirrel. Now that was nutty, wasn't it!" He laughed and continued, "He brought me different colored caramel corn and left me a note saying it was my favorite. I didn't know it was my favorite. I was awake when he came, and I heard footsteps, not hopping." I said, "I bet the Easter Bunny knows how to take little steps." He simply replied, "Grandma, I know the difference between hopping and walking. The Easter Bunny just sent a helper dressed in a bunny suit to deliver my presents and hide eggs."

Recipes Not Formulas!

Different children lead to different adventures. I tell these stories of my children and grandchildren to demonstrate both the kinds of captivating interactions one can have with children as well as to show how each interaction is a product of the personalities and inclinations of both adult and child. We are different people with different people. There really is such a thing as chemistry between people and no two sets of people will have the same kinds of experiences together. This is wonderful news because it means that although we can have recipes to have fun together, we never need to have formulas. Think of the recipes for fun in this book as a starting point where your unique self gets to add the ingredients and the measurements and the cooking time.

PART 2

ADVENTURES WITH IMAGINATION AND ENCHANTMENT

Imagination is more important than knowledge. For knowledge is limited to all we know and understand, while imagination embraces the entire world, and all there ever will be to know and understand.

~ EINSTEIN

CHAPTER 4

FINDING YOUR UNIQUE PATH
TO MAGICAL MOMENTS

One of the biggest motivations for me writing this book was to encourage early connections of time spent together with children that is lighthearted and full of love and wonder. The more we explore and take time with children, the more we are blessed in the richness of heart treasures. These shared moments are like hands full of diamonds plucked from shimmering waters as we navigate through the rivers of life with them.

I've listed a number of ways to engage children to help them learn while spending time with them. Encouraging curiosity in their worlds is an excellent skill to cultivate. And, of course, using all of their five senses and feelings increases the richness. With young children, if you add in the playfulness of the fairies and elves, you may find the children's desire and attention span in both moments and interests increases. When interests are piqued, exploring seems to take on a life of its own, and moments can slip pleasantly into minutes and hours.

Bringing in elves and fairies is a fun way to help a child interact with nature and get curious about the world around them. Do I feel the only way to establish these qualities is to have the elves and fairies a part of their lives? Absolutely not. But I do feel they are great helpers who easily capture children's interest and imaginations.

If a child starts learning at an early age about a wide variety of connections and interests, they will naturally be inclined to explore. Think about rocks. If you have never been introduced to them with names, what they might be used for, their beauty, and/or their differences, then you may look over the ground without interest. You may just see the ground. If your interest has been piqued as a child and encouraged, you will look at the ground and see a whole universe of things to think about and examine. Here's another example. For some, a tree is a tree without a name or a personality. To an outdoor explorer, it's a challenge to know their names and their differences, what makes each one and each species unique. This can be a game to start at an early age, to really see the variety in nature around us and to get to know the names and properties of each realm of the natural kingdom. If this is done on a playful, investigative level, this way of learning becomes a part of children as they mature. They will use this skill of seeing in greater detail throughout their lives.

Children are a lot like computers. What you download in them becomes their motherboard for how they live much of their lives. What is being downloaded: hope or despair? Feeling loved and important versus feeling insignificant? Positive self-esteem versus feeling not okay or not worthwhile? Creative versus more contained? Healthy reserves versus exhaustion or brick walls? Vivacious versus subdued? This list can go on and on, but the quality of time spent with children can have a significant effect on the way they expect how the world will treat them and how they will treat themselves. People generally seek what is familiar. They rely on their learned ways of interacting. This can include ways of feeling and expressing themselves, the types of people they gravitate towards, and ways of interacting or not interacting in life. People make choices with their conscious and subconscious minds. Having states of being, feeling, and sensing that are refreshing and revitalizing are huge gifts that can continue to blossom throughout a person's life.

Imagine your thoughts, desires, and paradigms as magnets; as they go out into the world, they can attract many of the same energetic potentials. With each positive, life-affirming and creative interaction you have with children, you are adding to their treasure trove of resources to call upon in the future. An established support system of love, patience, and acceptance may be the most important gift we can give to children. This gift is given gradually and is supported with positive interactive time.

EXPLORING YOUR INNATE GIFTS: YOUR BRIDGE TO CONNECTING WITH THE CHILDREN IN YOUR LIFE

What are your own natural inclinations and abilities?

Supportive, interactive time with children needs to be fun for both adult and child. If it is not fun for you, then it is not going to be much fun for the little ones. It's not a job. It's not work. Fun is fun. And the place to find fun is through expressing your own natural talents and gifts.

I oftentimes find many of us don't even realize how many special gifts we have to share. It is easy to look at hobbies and activities, but harder to see our own natural abilities or ways of being in the world as gifts. Below is a list of what I see as potential brilliance and interests. Once you start looking at this list, I'm sure you will recognize many of your own gifts.

(Please note, you will find many of these ideas intertwined in stories and adventures throughout this book. I thought it would be nice to have a more complete reference list in one place when you are thinking about what adventure might fit into a day or moment in time with your child/children.)

Locating Your Own Gifts and Talents:

A love for cooking. Even two-year-olds can stir, make messes, and do taste tests. My kids and grandkids have loved making up their own concoctions. Granted, in the beginning, many of them look and taste like Halloween experiments, but none of that dampens the joy in their creative hearts. I sometimes wonder if part of the appeal is doing something that seems grown up without someone monitoring how you are doing it. Or is it the doing itself? Would this be a combination of budding independence and creativity?

Creating themed meals, including decorating the table, maybe dressing the part, and adding information about different cultures can lead themselves to many a discussion and a feeling of being transported into another world for a brief time.

🍃 A love for reading books. The love of reading is an excellent joy to instill in children.

🍃 A talent as a visual artist. My husband is an artist. He shares his talents and patience with our grandchildren. Here is my macho husband drawing many a fairy, elf, and unicorn for many intriguing hours. Greyson, when he was four years old, came up with a layout plan for a family ranch which included equipment, and, of course, many a cow. He worked alongside Grandpa Jim for about two hours creating this masterpiece. Someone looked at the concept drawing and said, "Looks like your grandfather is a very good artist." Greyson looked back at them and promptly proclaimed, "I am also one of the artists here!" They have continued to combine their artistic abilities for hours on end whenever they are together, or on FaceTime across the miles.

🍃 Maybe your talent is you love children and they gravitate to you for hours of fun and carefree laughter. This may well be one of the best talents; children know you see them, enjoy them, and can feel you engage with them with all your heart and express it freely with smiles and laughter.

🍃 Plain enthusiasm is captivating.

🍃 Are you the type of person that loves games? It's a great way to spend time with children of all ages. Cards and chess can be life lifelong enjoyments. Board games these days are plentiful and there's one for every interest. Or puzzles, anyone?

🍃 Swimming, water skiing, jet skiing, surfing? Love of the open water can be a great adventure to share with children.

 Do you love the out-of-doors, in general, filled with hiking, biking, golf, tennis, camping, and fishing? Most kids love these types of experiences while having the added gift of creating these adventures with you. If we are hiking in the Rim Rocks by our house, the girls love to scale the rocky inclines. This will have me at the bottom ready to catch them, while Grandpa Jim, in his wisdom, is saying, "Step back, Honey, they will be just fine." And I do step back once they are standing on solid ground.

Do you love maps and travel? It is never too early to start teaching and inspiring, as my daughter-in-law Jenny showed me one day. A friend of mine had returned from Africa and had texted me some of her pictures. I was showing Madi, age two at the time, a picture of an elephant. I pointed at it and simply said, "Elephant." Jenny looked over, and said, "That is an elephant, and it lives in Africa, which is a continent. Can you say, 'Africa, continent, and elephant?'" The next thing I knew she was showing this two-year-old where Africa was located on the map. Needless to say, I was impressed, and a bit in disbelief; I couldn't imagine a two-year-old would understand much of what she was saying. With this type of ongoing, early training, Madi, now at age 16, has a love of maps, where places are located, and good bits of knowledge about many countries, continents, and their peoples. Traveling outside the United States is certainly on her bucket list.

Do you thrive on working with plants and flowers? For children, creating flower pots, fairy gardens, and learning how to take care of a variety of plants and flowers can be of interest.

Do you enjoy building? Kids love to plan and make things. At this time in my life, I wish my dad would have thought of taking the time to pass on some of his many talents to me. He was an excellent carpenter and could build anything; he built our house to perfection. He was a finishing cement worker and mechanically he enjoyed a good challenging puzzle of a needed repair. People often think of their skills and talents as adult pursuits but the children in your life might relish working with you and learning from you. Or, on the topic of wood, does anyone know how to whittle?

How about winter engagements? If it snows in your area, building snowmen, snow forts, and igloos, having snowball fights, or making snow angels can be exhilarating and challenging. Do you love downhill or cross-country skiing, snowboarding, sledding, or snowshoeing?

You may use your ingenuity with creating different crafts with children. The sky is the limit in terms of what the two of you might come up with.

Knitting, when passed along, brings gratifying memories of the time spent together as the years pass as well as the skill. While watching their nimble fingers creating, I've heard several friends' heartfelt stories relayed about the time spent with mothers, grandmothers, and friends who took the time to teach them this skill. I believe a hint of the love and memories of those earlier times are knitted into each new project my friends are inspired to create.

And what about that sewing machine? If you love to sew or even if you used to love to sew, it's time to revisit fabric and needle and thread. What could be more fun than making clothes, carrying cases, and quilts? And helping little fingers move the needle in and out of the fabric to make a new creation can lead to a lifetime of creative and practical outcomes.

With creative decorating, the sky is the limit when involving children. What ideas can they come up with for their bedrooms and playrooms? One friend's grandmother loved to create beauty in her home. My friend, Rosina, said you could even open closets and they would be like works of art. Her mother learned these skills and my friend grew up surrounded by both of these creative women who passed their knowledge and love of their artistry on to her. Rosina is a renowned, inventive, interior decorator that has blessed and enriched the lives of many.

Do you have a knowledge and love of music? What a gift to introduce children to different types of music, instruments, and musicians.

Concerts or events in the parks, anyone?

Being silly and dancing in the kitchen brings many lively moments of merriment.

🍃 Adventures can take place anywhere: a backyard, on a walk, or by simply jumping into a book for an arm chair vacation where imaginations soar.

🍃 Do you have a love of antiques, their history and their value?

🍃 The creativeness of photography is a lifelong skill and a beautiful way of learning to look at the world from different artistic perspectives.

🍃 Garage sale hunting (A.K.A. yard sales) is a great way to spend time with children. It is like a real treasure hunt with the magic of exploration flying with you!

🍃 Exercise? Rise and shine time to head off to the gym or yoga classes when any of the grandchildren are visiting. I love having them in class and joining me for what is a regular part of my life. The girls love going to class with me, and the instructors enjoy having their occasional visits.

🍃 Anyone a history buff?

🍃 Metal detecting is full of intrigue. My mom would have the grandkids out for hours metal detecting while the fires of adventure and anticipation flowed freely as they talked about possibilities of rare discoveries.

🍃 How about coin collecting?

🍃 Is juggling a talent of yours, or perhaps you are great at yo-yos? How about hula hooping? How about kite flying?

🍃 What about rock collecting? Have you ever thought of getting a small tumbler and bringing your favorite stones into glowing works of artful aliveness? By simply washing different stones in your collection, you will find their beauty come to life before they dry. By tumbling them, they will keep their enhanced luster, wet or dry.

When my mom and dad were on trips to the mountains, they collected unusual rocks for the flower garden area. I can remember over time hearing my mom say to my dad, "August, what do you think about this one?" Or my dad would be casually exploring by a stream and I would hear him saying, "Hey Clara, this one is really different." That would have us kids running to see what my dad had discovered. While walking with my mom in their garden, she could tell story after story about the different adventures to the mountains where they would find unusually beautiful rocks which they brought home. I don't think she went as far as naming them, but they all had their rightful places among the flowers.

Being a good listener. This is an excellent talent of warmth and caring. And it is easy to make interesting games out of listening. Being adventurous is definitely an advantage and gift to bring to others.

The grandkids will do most anything: walking in the neighborhood, hiking on trails, swimming, frolicking at the trampoline park, and riding bikes, just to mention a few. Greyson, now age five, was here this last summer for a week. We did a lot of bike riding in our neighborhood. He was testing his budding daredevil skills by riding back and forth over rocks between the road and sidewalk. I can tell you I was holding my breath and squelching the strong messages that wanted to pop out of my mouth as protective warnings. At one point, he was on the sidewalk, and I was on the street. He looked at me and said, "Grandma, come over here with me." I quickly assessed the situation, and with great hesitation in my heart, but with a smile on my face, I biked across the grass on the slight hill and popped up next to him. He rewarded me with the biggest of grins on his glowing face, and shouted, "Now that's my girl!"

In writing this book, I realized imagination and playfulness are a couple of my abilities. I had never really thought of them this way, as abilities, but that is what they are. With that in mind, look a little closer at your talents or ways of being that are assets in what comes easiest to you in life. Because they are easy, they are easy to miss; they may be what you do without thinking.

After you do your own assessment of your gifts and talents as well as your areas of expertise and interests, you may want to enlist your friends and relatives to help expand your vision of yourself. Take a poll among those who love you and find out the qualities that come to mind when they think about you. You may be tickled by their unique vision of the gifts that you have shown to them which you may not even be aware of. How fun is that?!

Also, take a moment and let yourself contemplate which ideas of enjoyment you might be inspired to add to your life or to playful times with children in your life. This might be something you and the child in your life might learn and explore together. Now that sounds like mischief and laughter in the making.

CHAPTER 5

ELVES, FAIRIES, AND THEIR EXUBERANT NATURES

This chapter is about how you yourself can introduce elves and fairies and other enchanting concepts into the lives of children. The magical thinking stage is a childhood developmental stage that begins at about age two years old up to age seven, and, of course, lightheartedly beyond that up to old age—if we are lucky! It is considered a completely normal stage and necessary for children's development. Many children store the memory and continued gifts of brushstrokes of enchantment from this early stage in life. They can bring out the magic from this time to be used in their adult lives. Think of writers, poets, artists, designers, and photographers, to name a few, who continue to be gifted with the creativity of seeing beyond the ordinary.

Since this book originated from adults questioning me about ideas for whimsical interactions with children involving the elves and fairies, I thought it only fair to start out with some of the fairies' and elves' attributes and ways of being from my perspective. You will find others scattered throughout this book. I would like to reassure you, I don't believe there are any hard and fast rules about what fairies and elves are like, what they are interested in, when they are close by, or how to have them a part of one's imaginative life. You can add anything whimsical or wonderful to these attributes and descriptions that fits you and the child you are sharing with. Combine your creativity and curiosity with that of a child's, and you will find you have a recipe that brings joy and pleasant riches to your hearts and memories. I love how flights of fancy can help enhance the experiences and interactions between children and grownups.

PLEASE NOTE: I haven't branched out to other characters like gnomes, hobbits, or characters like the Tooth Fairy. Our hands and hearts have been filled up with the lore and playfulness of the elves, fairies, plus a dose of the leprechauns and unicorns here and there. You may have your own special relationships with these magical characters. So, let your imagination take flight and enjoy. Take notice of thoughts, images, or memories that may pop up for you.

You may be returning to the question of, "Why engage with the idea of these whimsical characters at all?" So here are some gifts and benefits of doing so.

Gifts from Indulging in the Mystique of the Wee People:

⚹ Entertaining exploration of diverse environments and habitats.

⚹ A love and respect for the environments around you and the child.

⚹ Sharing and giving to others.

⚹ Expanded learning and interests.

⚹ Increasing vocabularies at a young age.

⚹ Relating to adults in playful ways.

⚹ Really enjoying the treasures of the magical thinking stage.

⚹ Increasing an ability to easily and fully be very aware in the present moment.

⚹ Maintaining a good dose of curiosity.

⚹ Participating in an abundance of warm-hearted connections and memories from childhood.

⚹ Developing the framework and skills to increase possibilities beyond what is presented.

⚹ Feeling valued; feeling love, protection, and hope.

⚹ Adult(s) and child/children will have formed special bonds around the wee folk complete with secret musings around the adventures shared by their hearts.

A lovely part of all of these ideas is they seem to magically transition into maturing, refined, supportive values and ways of engaging in life. Developing interests, passions, activities, relationships, and wisdoms will be avenues which help children in navigating the ups and downs of life with increased ease and agility.

HOW TO INTRODUCE THE IDEA OF THE FAIRIES & ELVES INTO THE MAGICAL THINKING STAGE

Introducing the idea of the fairies and elves can be quite simple. If the child grows up with the idea of the wee characters, you just continue on. If the child is two-plus years, the introduction can be as simple as reading a children's book, seeing a movie, cartoon, or a fun painting which includes the elves and fairies. There are many stories and bits of information in this book you can read to your child that will amusingly introduce these characters into their lives. If a child asks if they are real, you can easily say something like, "I love the idea of them. Let's watch for clues." When watching for clues, you may say, "I may have seen something out of the corner of my eye" or "I think I heard" or "Do you think...?" Statements like these encourages imaginations to be on high alert.

Other ways of introduction could be having a little fairy or elf popping into their life to sit on their dresser, or one they can enjoy.

It is also easy to pick a visual sign such as seeing isolated pieces of tall grass or weeds swaying. It oftentimes starts with me saying something like, "Oh, I think I saw something! It could be one of those mischievous characters waving at us and letting us know they are around!" Or sometimes: "Did you hear that...it might have been a little elf bell...Listen."

Fairies and elves like to surprise others by creating special scenes in the woods, a yard, or in a park. You might see a little flower popping up early in the spring, a little rainbow cascading over a glimmering creek, or a mushroom edging its way up from under a fallen branch. For me, these sightings fall under the category of remarkable gifts of wonder. All it may take is you saying, "This might be some clever fairy with a fun-loving heart that waved his or her wand," or you can say, "See the work of the artistic elf who painted that rainbow." And watch how your own heart grows in delight!

One surprise by the fairies that is easy to spot are "fairy rings" that seem to magically appear in lawns. Fairy rings are circular areas that appear in lawns that are abnormal growths generally where there are high levels of organic matter. Given their mysterious circular designs, they have been mystically of interest since ancient times. I still find myself visualizing whimsical characters dancing and flying around in these circles while being captured by some unknown intrigue. I am delightfully entertained with lively pictures of the diversity in their dress, wings, and hair ornaments. I love being pulled into these imaginative moments.

As children mature, they naturally grow out of the younger magical thinking stage, but they can still hold the inclination for seeing mysteries in their worlds. So luckily, we have the adventures of the likes of Harry Potter or other books or films to fill these delights and engagements in imagination and creation.

When Madi was about 11 years old, she asked me, "Are you the one that brings my fairy and elf presents?" I looked at her and said, "Do you really want to know?" She said, "I'm not sure. Let me think about it." Later that day, she said she guessed she would like to know. I let her know I bring some of them. She said, "Which ones?" I replied, with a smile, "That, I'm not telling."

You see, it happened that, Jenny, Madi's mom, was great at welcoming the elves and fairies into Madi's and Jessie Bean's world with Jenny's own added twists. Those additions included notes, surprises, checking for fairy wings, and doing her creative part in carrying on the aliveness of imagination and enchantment for as long as possible with the girls. Knowing this, you can say I was telling Madi the truth when I said that I bring some of them!

A week after I admitted my part in supporting these elusive characters, Madi said, "Grandma, I've been thinking. Now that I know, I can start leaving presents and notes for Jessie Bean." (Jessie Bean is six years younger than Madi.) "It is going to be so much fun." Madi took this to heart and over the past five years she has gifted Jessie Bean many treasures of notes from the fairies and elves, teachings of their lore from Madi's point of view, involving Jessie Bean in play in "fairy and elf land" in their back yard which included and gifts from the fairies and elves. Madi had a number of little fairies and elves that magically decided to relocate to Jessie Bean's room. Mitzi was the last of the fairies that flew into Jessie Bean's welcoming wonderland. I sometimes ponder if Mitzi didn't fly there by herself; I'm not sure how easy it would have been for Madi to give up such a treasured, lifelong friend.

Now that Jessie Bean will be 11 this summer, she and Madi are going to start these traditions with three little neighbor girls. The twins are almost two years old, and their sister is four years old. The love of creating and giving continues on.

ATTRIBUTES OF THE FAIRIES AND ELVES

ENCHANTMENT ALERT! Below you will find some of my imaginings of the fairies and elves. Please enjoy and see what flights of imaginations you find yourself thinking up.

Fairy Wings

The wings of a fairy can change depending on the weather, where they are going, or just because. I can talk a long time about fairy wings. An example would be imagining with the child what winter wings would look like—they could be constructed out of snow crystals. When the sun hits them just right, tiny rainbows of color are delicately illuminated. Fairies use so many things as part of their artistry in decorating their wings: from sparkles caught on the water to flowers to colors borrowed from rainbows or the colors in the environment around them to dewdrops. They use about anything that catches their eye. You can have a child draw different fairy wings, and you may enjoy drawing with them. Some fairies like to do things like decorating their wings differently on opposing sides or differently on the front than the back. They think it's comical and creative.

Fairies may also make wings out of flowers in the winter or display snowflake wings in the summer. Imagine fairies flying through a fluffy snowstorm touting multicolored, flowered wings, or imagine them modeling gorgeous snowflake wings as they fly though the heat on a summer's day.

Checking for Growing Fairy Wings on Children

If you have never checked for growing fairy wings on children, it's simple. Have them turn around with their back facing you and feel where they may be sprouting a pair of their own wings. You will find the clues by touching their shoulder blades on the edges. Children will then feel the possibilities. Have them move these bones back and forth like fluttering their wings. The feeling of having wings is quite impressive, I would say.

At times, I will still ask my 10-year-old granddaughter on the phone how her wings are growing. The next to the last time I asked, she said, "Just a minute," and she asked her mom to check. This last time when I asked her, she said, "Let's FaceTime, and you can let me know what they look like." I stepped up to the challenge, which had her quite happy that she was touting such impressive, inspiring wings.

If you are really good at visualizing fairy wings, give a look or feel to see if you have them too. You might be surprised!

Discovering Fairy Wands

Fairy wands are quite curious given the mystique around them. I imagine the wands are as varied in their usage as the fairies themselves. Wands might be utilized to add extra brilliance to diverse scenes such as cold, frosty winter mornings. Or the glistening in splashing droplets of water as it tumbles and slides down a substantial waterfall in the sunlight—this may be the work of fairies with their special wands. Start looking around and you might discover other scenes that may have been artistically touched by their seemingly unending supply of fairy wand dust.

With a light touch of a fairy wand, diamond-like dewdrops, intricate snowflakes, small rainbows, colorful berries, and remarkable little flowers can be preserved for later use in decorating their wings or putting them in their hair. Can you imagine delicate, light as air, snowflake wings decorated with small, red berries and tiny blue forget-me-not flowers interlaced around the edges to complete a vision of magic? The patterns and usage of the preserved treasures from the fairies' environments are as endless as one's imagination.

The list of what fairies do with their wands goes on and on. There are all sorts of captivating possibilities waiting to be discovered.

Interesting Personalities

Fairies and elves are widely known for their consistent attributes of kindness and joy. On the other hand, they have a great flair for being mischievous, high-spirited, and they delight in humor. They love to surprise others and love to be the recipient of surprises. They do have big hearts, and they like adventures.

Diversity in Feelings

Fairies and elves are great at feeling all their feelings. Yes, they can get fearful, angry, disgusted, guilty, confused, weak, or sad, as well as feeling happy and joyful or surprised. They start learning at an early age how to deal with their feelings and they love to learn new words that express feelings. They actually believe the highest level of magic is simply real feelings. You will discover a list of words to express a variety of feelings on pages 157 & 158. It is an art form to be able to express feelings with a fine-tuned range of descriptive words and accompanying body language and facial expressions.

Elves and fairies love feelings. I can see, with a touch and sprinkle of fairy dust in the air, how a person might suddenly realize something uniquely special about themselves that makes their hearts genuinely happy for an instant. Pay attention when it seems that you have been gifted with a feeling of light-heartedness. Our memories and being totally engaged in the moment can prompt the same types of experiences.

Water Sports with the Elves and Fairies

Racing in the water can be one or more of the wee people having an exuberant ride downstream on branches, flowers, ducks, or boats made out of shells or tree bark. You understand, they will use anything that floats—they are creative little characters. I've heard that some of them love to race downstream while seeing who can turn the most circles or slide over or under obstacles like tree trunks or well planted spider webs. The webs are especially tricky. If any of the wee people get too close, they

may end up with a boat partner with more legs than they care to count. But no need to be worried, they are actually friends with the spiders.

Analyzing Snow Crystals

On a sunny snow day, if you take a few extra minutes to analyze the snow, you may find the surface covered with gifts of brilliantly shining fairy sparkles. On very special days, sparkles turn into tiny glistening rainbows. The end result will be smiling hearts for all who take the time to explore. It is a mystery as to when this will happen, but it is worth developing an investigative spirit and trained eye for these dramatic occurrences. This is a lot like catching an awe-inspiring sunrise or sunset.

Elves' and Fairies' Favorite Leaves

The elves and fairies pick out their special leaves and start contemplating how they are going to uniquely color them as touches of fall begin to transform different environments. You see, with the last of their crystals from the year before, they love to help Jack Frost with his tumbling kaleidoscope of designs in changing the seasons from late summer into the bustling fall. This includes designing and coloring many of the various leaves in this season.

Riding the Leaves in the Fall and Flying Through the Forest

As these artistic fall leaves set sail on windy days down creeks, over rolling hills, and up and down bustling streets, you can be sure some of them carry the artists who creatively blessed them with one-of-a-kind designs. The wind is the wee people's friend in these adventures as it will often times send the leaves up for extra rides by lifting them high in the sky, over trees and bushes with artful weaving and tumbling agility. I know if some of the more mischievous fairies are around, I can see they might add in a bit of fairy dust to enhance those fantastic rides.

This is a bit silly, but elves love to stand on a branch and have several of their friends stretch the branch backwards to its max. As the friends release this bough of energy, the elf will fly through the forest with the greatest of ease and merriment with quick nods to their friends as they fly by in a blur. A wee bit of celebration passes through forests or parks on these lively days of adventures. By this time, I would imagine, you might find signs of these types of events especially on windy days.

Disappearing

These wee characters love the fact that people are curious about them, but they learn from a young age not to be seen.

When people are approaching, they love to wait until the last second to disappear. At those times, you let the child know you may have seen something. You can search with the child for clues, such as when a leaf or two will come playfully floating to the ground. It's a good possibility an elf or fairy is exuberantly catching a lazy ride on its dance to the ground.

A Game of Jumping-In to an Imaginary World

Another way to gain some insight into the worlds of elves and fairies is to have an adventure with the child or children in your life. Get yourselves seated or stand comfortably wherever you are, close your eyes, and while holding hands, count to three and pretend to jump into paintings, imagined environments, books, or your backyard, for starters. And just as quickly, open your eyes and start pretending you are a fairy or an elf in these different scenes. Pay close attention to details that might be clues. What do they think would intrigue the fairies and elves? You may find children are so taken by this idea, they will get up and start flying or jumping about with boundless energy. You will probably find, if you set the scene, the children will paint in most of the rest of the imaginary adventures without much prompting from you.

Try visualizing yourselves as a tiny wee character sitting on top of a flower, riding on a bird, or sitting on a branch.

This idea may find you imagining sitting on a bright orange poppy in the spring or a beautiful rose in the heat of summer. What would it be like to be sitting on this gift of beauty from nature? Gently feel the softness of the petals. How would it feel if the wind was blowing and you were riding in the flower? Describe all the sensations, the wind, what you see, the smells. The view could be quite magical looking out from being perched on a flower or branch.

Maybe you fancy a ride in the water on a lily pad or fly into the intricate elf and fairy village in a forest. Laughter and intrigue will float in and out of these exchanges of imagination.

THINGS THAT GLISTEN, SPARKLE, AND SHINE

ENCHANTMENT ALERT!
Unicorn Snot

Jessie Bean came by this jar of dazzling, really slimy gel-type unicorn snot as a gift from one of the fairies one morning. At this point, you may be saying, who would give or want a jar of snot? Well, you have to remember the unicorns are special friends of the fairies and elves, and anything from them must be a great gift. Either way, you can imagine how she felt when she first found the present. She eventually overcame the idea of putting her fingers in the clear, light-green slimy substance and found out when she did, her fingers rather magically had a glittery sparkle that appeared. She assumed this was added by the fairies. Once she got past this rather disgusting idea of putting snot on her face, it became her favorite addition when she was going somewhere special or to school on most mornings. She thinks of it as magical, based on her observation that her dad doesn't tell her to go in and wash it off while adding the famous little lecture, "You aren't old enough to wear anything that looks like makeup." She says she isn't sure her dad can even see it. She surmises that he isn't really aware of the elves and fairies, now that he is all grown up.

Campfires and Campsites

Fairies and elves are intrigued by campfires; they love how the light of the fire dances with the drama of the strikingly starlit nights. On those moody nights while sitting close to a campfire, you might hear twigs dancing and tossing in the wind, tiny crunches on the ground, trees rubbing against each other, or little animals making sounds. You may assume that the creatures of the forest may be visiting with the elves or fairies.

If an outside fire isn't available, consider setting up one in the backyard while camping out or a campfire substitute in your house. Be creative. If you don't have logs and twigs, roll up some newspapers or magazines and cover them in brown paper. Next find a good lighting source like flashlights or self-lighting candles that flicker. You now have the beginnings of a campsite. Add a few treats such as hot dogs and s'mores, a few chairs or blankets to sit on, and start telling stories. Depending on the age of the child, entertaining ghost stories have been told around many a campfire. If this is overnight, don't forget the sleeping bags for indoors or out-of-doors.

Fireflies

Fireflies are great friends with the fairies and elves and another source of whimsical light. If you are lucky enough to live where they also live, you can see them in the forest creating shimmering designs with their lights gently blinking on and off. They may spend an evening adding special lighting to a fairy's wings or an elf's shoes. One of the favorite times for the elves and fairies is when the fireflies light up a cascading waterfall on a pitch-dark night. On these occasions, it's told the fish will oftentimes start jumping into the rainbows of lights, and with a slight nod to the wee characters, they will suddenly disappear back into the cover of the night and churning waters.

Glow-In-The-Dark Paint

Fairies and elves are attracted by things that glow in the dark. There is paint that glows in the dark that is made for outside. If you have a little door on a tree or a fence you could paint it with this unusual paint for the fun of it.

Prisms in a Window

Prisms definitely establish some elements of surprise and curiosity. My children and grandchildren have all received prisms and crystals as presents from the elves and fairies. You can spend a whole afternoon chasing rainbows, telling stories, and imagining the diverse characters who are drawn to such complex beauty.

Rainbows

A special gift is when you spot a rainbow. A well-known fact is when rainbows are around, you can bet there are elves and fairies romping in these dramatic creations of enjoyment. Jumping on a color in a rainbow and taking a breezy ride across the sky is exhilarating for them. Maybe you will find them tasting the delicious colors. Fairies are known for grabbing bits of color to add to their fairy wings, and elves are exceptionally creative with adding these colors to their stockings and the inside of their elf shoes. If you ever get a chance, inspect the artistry in these little characters' stockings and shoes. They consider colors magical given they can inspire feelings.

Also, you probably all know the leprechauns are famous for their mischievous entrances into these rainbow scenes. Leprechauns are the ones to watch closely because they are the ones who, like the rascals they are, swipe the pots of gold when you are getting close to the end of rainbows. Now, think about it, would you rather have the pot of gold or have the knowledge the leprechauns are quietly close by?

Watch carefully, you may find you can spot all sizes of rainbows in a number of places.

Balloons and Kites

Elves and fairies are fascinated by balloons and kites. They love to hitch rides on the balloons as they dance higher and higher into the welcoming sky. These wee people have the same love and curiosity with kites. They are fascinated by all the bright colors, speed, and dipping and diving actions. You can imagine how an expert kite flyer might be stunned at the amusing, out-of-control personality his kite takes on when one of the wee people decides to hitch a ride.

Drones

In this new day and age with the addition of drones, I imagine elves and fairies will be finding them of interest. I can quite

imagine them popping on a drone and mischievously guiding and flying it across the sky with its owner being completely perplexed and a little frustrated.

Bubbles

Elves and fairies are mesmerized by bubbles, these delicate bits of shimmering rainbows of various shapes and sizes. The idea of riding in or on one of them is always a fun game since the bubbles can disappear about as fast as any little elf or fairy. This brings in the idea of how much the fairies and elves love a challenge that tickles their sense of drama and humor. If you were graced with the opportunity to see them sitting on a tree branch or on the rail of a porch, you would probably see several of them laughing, tumbling around, and being plain silly while waiting for the next child (or adult) to blow some more bubbles. They are really taken by the tremendously large bubbles; they find the challenge of popping into one of them altogether exhilarating.

Frolicking in Water

Summer, kids, and water are a natural draw for the curious fairies and elves.

They love being around in the summer when kids are delighting in water adventures. You may find them leaping onto a waterslide and taking the first ride if someone is hesitant. They love the glistening sparkles created as a gift from the brilliant sun. As kids run through sprinklers, you can imagine the fairies flying in and around the sparkles as they rise to greet them. The elves can be seen jumping and splashing in the grass and sliding down anything that gets wet and ends in a pool of refreshing water.

St. Patrick's Day with the Leprechauns

ENCHANTMENT ALERT! "It's time to start setting up the traps to catch the leprechauns," Spencer encouraged his younger sister, Erika. He was as skilled as any seasoned Secret Service agent in pursuit of capturing his unsuspecting fugitive. You see, he had been honing his elaborate trap-setting talents for several years. You could see his mind beginning to work during the week before the eve of March 17th, as he imagined and devised ideas for this year's traps that were sure to catch one of those quick-witted tricksters. These mischievous leprechauns loved the challenges of springing his traps and not getting caught. They were very aware that the price of their freedom was to leave a gift in the trap.

Erika learned quickly, but I noticed during her younger years, part of her game plan was to trick her brother into setting lots of traps—many more than she set. She knew that she would share in whatever gifts were left in exchange for the leprechaun's freedom. By bedtime, with all the energy of anticipation swirling around, it was hard for anyone of us to settle. When I would kiss Erika on her beautiful face on those nights, I was sure I'd catch a little glimpse of a knowing smile. Was it satisfaction? Or maybe just the fun in knowing she had tricked her big brother a little, again, just like a tricky leprechaun might try?

The mornings always started in great excitement and disbelief. When we quickly went from room to room, there was no doubt the leprechauns had visited. We were all wide-eyed, and the kids looked at me to see if the leprechauns had overstepped their welcome this time. Why were they wondering if the leprechauns went too far? Things were a creative mess: big chairs were turned over, pictures on the walls were discombobulated, the water in the toilet bowls was green, cupboard doors were left ajar, there was a chair on the table, and our big decorative rooster was on top of the chair. It almost looked like it flew up there, to either get a better vantage point for the whirlwind happening or to plain get out of the way. Within a few seconds, after the shock of seeing the dramatic condition of our home wore off, both children seemed to be almost shot out of a cannon of thrilling intrigue as they scampered to the traps. Now they were moving fast but contained themselves as they slowly uncovered each and every trap. They knew if the leprechaun was still in the trap, it would disappear instantly. I did notice they never really put their faces too close to the traps. They weren't sure what kind of a surprise encounter might occur if one of the wee characters was captured and they popped out. Much to their delight— and disappointment—they always found things like money, shamrocks, glitter, little treats, and just about anything green was left behind. Once the enthralling excitement of the morning was waning, and things seemed to be getting back to normal, the surprises continued. When I poured the white milk into their favorite glasses, the milk turned green. They certainly savored this gift of drama for part of the morning. Then, when I made them pancakes, they also turned green. Oh, I forgot to mention, the first thing the kids did when waking was to put on something green. They knew tradition allows you to pinch someone who isn't wearing green on this day of celebration. I was thinking why that would be tradition? Of course, a leprechaun's favorite color is green, and the trick of a pinch would be their way of reminding everyone of their importance. My mom would always say, "We are just enough Irish to count." I have always figured it was a very good thing.

Tip for adults hoping to make some St. Patrick's Day fun: A drop of green food coloring is the trick supporting the magic of things like milk, toilet water, pancakes, and eggs turning green. Clandestinely add drops of coloring the night before to glasses, bowls, and pans. One year, my daughter-in-law Jenny didn't have any green food coloring left. Being a bright young woman, she put on her thinking cap and calculated the blue and yellow equation equaling green. So she put blue food coloring in the toilets, and when the girls went to the bathroom the next morning, the water actually turned green. What an ingenious mom.

Moving forward in time, two years ago, I was with Erika's son Greyson, my grandson, who was four years old at the time of that St. Patrick's Day. He was already spectacular at setting traps. We did briefly talk about the size of leprechauns the night before, and I let him know I thought they were in the range of about two to six inches tall or so. Later that same morning, after he had enthusiastically scampered to all of his traps with the anticipation of hope running strong that he might have snared one of the elusive wee ones, he asked if I had taken a shower yet. I said I hadn't and headed downstairs after a couple of minutes. As I opened the door, I ran into what seemed like a small snowstorm. I gathered up all of the tiny pieces of the white mystery. I believe they might have been constructed by some mischievous little hands from a couple of tissues. I went running upstairs and threw them up into the air, announcing the leprechauns had visited the bathroom downstairs. Everyone showed excitement with my discovery. When I was leaving to go home, Greyson came up to me and whispered, "Grandma, I was the one that left the surprise in your bathroom." I gave him an extra hug, and warmly whispered, "That's perfect. You surprised everyone!" And I ruffled up his hair, just a little.

A couple of days later, when I talked to him on the phone, he strongly stated, "Grandma, I saw the leprechaun, and he wasn't small." I asked what size the leprechaun was, and he simply stated, "Grandma, he's the size of a man!" I couldn't argue; I haven't totally seen one, just flashes of movement out of the

corner of my eye. I did tell him, "Well, it sounds like leprechauns come in all sizes." I did let him know there are lots of them rather than just one. I explained there is only one of the characters like the Sandman, Jack Frost, and Santa." He said, "Oh." And that was the end of that.

These types of heartfelt imaginings are gifts that can be woven into the recipes for inspiring different types of connections and curiosity with children. Hopefully you will find something new to explore, and, at the very least, you will build some delightful memories. Please note, most any of these adventures can happen nicely with or without the charm of the elves and fairies. The most important thing is that you are encouraging and teaching children how to explore their environments down to the smallest of details with trained eyes and open hearts.

PART 3

MAKING THE ORDINARY
EXTRAORDINARY WITH IMAGINATION
AND ENCHANTMENT

CHAPTER 6

PLEASURE AROUND MEALS, BAKING, AND PICNICS

Food is always an important part of our lives, and each snack and meal are opportunities for imaginative connections. Fancy that!

LEARNING TO SAVOR TASTES

When the grandchildren and I are out and about, we sometimes go to a small stand in the Baxter Hotel in Bozeman that sells elegantly designed small chocolates from France. They get to pick out one piece while knowing the choice is to either eat it in one bite or to take small bites and savor it to its fullest. Once six-year-old Jessie Bean learned about this choice, she made a one-inch square piece last a whole afternoon. Greyson, starting at four years old would say, "I know Grandma, I need to savor it."

I have a challenge for you: I would like you to savor something like a nice dinner, eating it slowly while really activating your senses. Next, try this same experiment with a child. They will be delighted by the interesting ways you draw them into the experience. They will probably surprise you with some of their own ideas. Ask them questions like: What is the best part of savoring the treat or meal? Describe the colors on your plate, and which are your favorites? Do colors taste? How do the foods taste in your mouth or feel in your mouth? What if you put two tastes in your mouth at the same time? What are the smells?

I found this a great way to learn more about children's likes and dislikes which helps you prepare foods for them that they will enjoy. At times, getting children to eat a well-balanced diet can be a bit of a struggle. Textures, colors, developing taste buds, emotions, and personalities are some of the components that come into play for mealtimes.

Ease and Enjoyment with Meals (Even If Eating is An Issue)

I've included a few simple ideas I discovered over time that may help if eating is an issue with children.

1. Being aware of simple likes and dislikes and incorporating them into meals in subtle ways that don't make a big deal out of it. What do I mean? If, for example, you find a child likes fresh carrots rather than cooked, it would be easy to have both of them at a meal. For a child, it might be the texture of the cooked carrots is disagreeable, or they just don't like them cooked. To me, it's more important to have them eating the vegetable, and gradually acquiring a taste for cooked ones. I know the idea of children eating the meal that is prepared for the family is wise. On the other hand, if the parent or grandparent is aware of the child's likes or dislikes, they can add them to the meal without having the child know the addition was actually added for them. Keep in mind how you would feel if someone was making you eat something you don't like.

2. The concept of trying "one" bite of a new food or a food they haven't tried in a long time is a great idea. Oftentimes they don't think it's in their best interest, and they resist. One thought would be to make a family game of exploration out of it. It could easily happen with "Who wants to be the first explorer tonight?" And that person can demonstrate by facial expressions and/or sounds as to how they like or dislike the food. If this becomes a family game, the child may oftentimes want to be the first explorer. This allows for laughter, ease, and engagement, and gives children a feeling of positivity around the idea of "one bite." It would be smart to jump in and be the first one trying the foods part of the time, while adding your own exaggerated impressions. Part of this game is everyone tries the food in question. This idea of exploring can replace much of the resistance around new foods.

3. Disappearing food. ENCHANTMENT ALERT! Fairies and elves enjoy most foods, but you don't hear too much about how they absolutely love fruits and vegetables. If you aren't careful, they might swipe food right off your plate when you aren't looking. This has happened to my kids. They would turn around and be talking, then turn back...and some of their food might be gone! Foods like broccoli, berries, carrots, mushrooms, or pieces of meat. If they didn't notice the food disappeared, I would say something like, "I thought you had more peas. I bet one of those elves or fairies took it. I know they love it." It was interesting how many of the swiped foods by the fairies or elves would soon become favorites of the children. You might read the first part of this paragraph to your child to set the scene.

4. Serving themselves their own food can make them feel like they are making their own choices. You can have a rule that you put a little of everything on your plate even if it is just one bite. You will be helping them some, but this will be worth the effort in the long run.

5. If children help to prepare foods, even if it is only stirring it, or adding some of the ingredients, they are more likely to try it. Lightly praise them for their contributions. Depending on the age of the child, you can easily say something like, "Jimmy practically made the salad [or sandwiches, fruit plate, or vegetables tray]. He worked so hard." Or: "Jimmy is great at mixing the salad. It is going to be extra special." In this vein, find a recipe cookbook for children and have them make some of their own foods.

It's fun to have a family recipe book with dishes and whole meals that the children love to eat and also help cook. It can be as simple as a three-ring binder notebook. The child can have the job of creating the recipe page or adding their illustrations for the recipe that you write down. What a precious legacy to have!

6. Some of the time, if possible, ask children what they would like prepared for a meal and this will naturally spur them on to enjoying their meal more. It may not be your first choice, but fair is fair.

9. Taking the attention off of the meal and engaging in family exchanges is oftentimes of benefit. There are a couple of word games or guessing games that might be fun additions at mealtimes to make eating an easy and fun process.

10. Every so often have a taste test night where you have variations of the same kind of food prepared in different ways. Everyone can rate which version is their favorite. You can also do this for take-out food by getting the same dish from different restaurants. You can even make up scorecards for each person if you have lots of different dishes to rate. The variations on this are endless, and the fun and memories will go on forever too!

SETTING THE STAGE FOR A FUN MEALTIME

Using the "Grandma Clara Dishes"

"Grandma, you can't forget we always get to use Grandma Clara dishes when we come to visit at your house. This always makes the meals and treats so special," Madi joyfully reminded me. (Grandma Clara is my mother.) I have "Dear Abby" to thank for this idea from years ago. It was something that made total sense to me. She wrote, "Why save things like special dishes and glasses just for company? Think about using them more often with the most special people in your life." And who is more special than children and grandchildren? I started employing this idea, by using the "Grandma Clara" dishes with Madi when she was small. The dishes have never been happier.

The Intrigue of Silver Spoons

At my house, I have a tiny, intricately-designed silver sugar spoon set. We, meaning the grandchildren and I, believe that they came from a Scottish castle. I purchased them used while in Scotland at a nice jewelry store. The fact that they were secondhand added to their mystery. Can you imagine the parties these fine silver pieces were involved in with the Queen and attendants? The grandchildren and I are quite intrigued about the history of these delicate mystery players in our lives. Their dainty size has us naturally savoring yummy small bites while we ponder their true, earlier adventures.

Elegant Glasses

I have a love for crystal glasses with long stems, and the grandchildren totally enjoy using them. If a parent catches us, they will dutifully remind the children to be very careful, and then they run over and try to teach them how to hold them. Up to this point, the grandchildren and I thought things were going perfectly. They have never broken anything, and if they did, oh well. Not a problem.

Unique Napkins

Jessie Bean has always loved setting the table when she visits. Her artful eye, which she has used from the young age of about five, loves picking out various beautifully-designed napkins to complete her gift of table presentations. This has in turn developed in me a keen eye for spotting new patterns, colors, and sizes for a variety of mood-setting napkins to add to her choices in her artistry of perfect touches.

COOKING

Missing Donuts

It's good to know fairies and elves love the happiness, the smells, and the anticipation of confections popping out of the oven or off the stove. One of their favorites is when homemade donuts are in the making. When I was young, upon occasion, Mom would make cake donuts. We had bags of cinnamon sugar, powdered sugar, and bowls of frosting waiting for these famous treats to pop out of the bubbling oil. Besides the donuts, the other elements that made these events special were a number of kids in the neighborhood seemed to have excellent timing for when these happenings began, and they added to the business, laughter, and enjoyment of the mouthwatering confections when they graced our home. Mom shared with everyone—and I'm sure the elves and fairies were first in line for these noted events.

Here is the recipe as it appeared in my mom's cookbook:

SWEET MILK DOUGHNUTS

3 eggs	½ teaspoon nutmeg
1 cup sugar	3½ cups sifted flour
2 tablespoons shortening	1 cup milk
3 teaspoons baking powder	½ teaspoon lemon extract
1 teaspoon salt	

Beat eggs until very light, beat in sugar, then add melted shortening. Sift baking powder, salt and nutmeg with 1 cup flour and stir into first mixture alternately with milk. Add lemon extract and just enough flour to make a very soft dough. Chill. Roll out to ¾ inch thick on a lightly floured board. A soft dough makes light, tender doughnuts when cooked. Fry in deep fat oil (360 to 370 degrees F.) and drain on unglazed paper. Makes 2 dozen.

The recipe that we used came out of an old cookbook of my Mom's that no longer has a front or back cover on it for identifying information. At the end of the book, there was a section on "War Time Cookery" which I thought was interesting. Please enjoy this historical family recipe in your own home with friends and family!

A Taffy Pull

I want to put a special emphasis on taffy pulls because it is something my mom had suggested on a number of occasions, including when I was a teenager. I am sad to say, I never took her up on her offer. This is one of my small regrets. But my husband, Jim, was fortunate enough to have participated in this totally fun activity when he was growing up. Oh, and in case, you have never heard of a taffy pull, it's a candy that you make on your stove that needs to be pulled once it is set out to cool.

He talked about how hot the taffy was when you started pulling it with another person and how your arms would get exhausted. You see, you need to pull the taffy until it cools down and is nice and soft before the candy is at the point of perfection. Plus, he reminisced about how there was always a lot of laughing and talking in a bright kitchen with many smells dancing and swirling around, cementing the events in a special place in all their memories.

Well, after thinking about it and feeling sad that I missed out on the taffy pull, I decided that I should give it a try. Jessie Bean was eager to help out. And even Jim was there to lend his strong hands. First, we experimented with a 100-year-old recipe that didn't quite work—too lumpy. But then we found another recipe and had so much fun making it and pulling it that we've already made three batches with different flavors. I guess we can now call ourselves experts! And something tells me that the next time we make it, the rest of the family might want to give their muscles a workout pulling the cooling taffy. A quick Internet search for salt water taffy will lead you to lots of recipes. Have fun experimenting and finding one that works for you.

Cracking Eggs with the Kids

This is great fun. The first step is to see if the child has any interest in learning this new skill. I have never had a "no" or even a "well maybe." When I've asked this question, an enthusiastic "Yes" would find us both darting to the sink to wash our hands. Every child I've taught thought we might leave out the hand washing step. But this step lent itself to a short lesson in why it's always important when handling food…boring, unless you get sidetracked with bubbles! In preparation, I would have a couple dozen eggs on hand. With the stool up to the sink, our hands washed, the lessons would begin. In my mind, this experience was the beginning step in the journey of creating self-reliant cooks. I've done this with my children and grandchildren when they turned three. It is now a traditional rite of passage in our family. I can't say the parents were always as pleased with this step towards independence, given the grandchildren would often times tell me their mom or dad will only let them crack eggs occasionally. I get it, parents have time constraints. But I find myself being about as disappointed as the grandkids when they don't get to use their newfound skills on a more regular basis. The other thought parents have had is it seems wasteful to throw away one or two dozen eggs. My thought is they are learning a new skill, and who doesn't practice when learning? I'm sure you could use the eggs for something, but that would deprive the children of the experience of trying to extradite small broken pieces of eggshell out of the bowl and away from the clinging, slippery egg whites with their little fingers. I know a spoon can work well, but developing a respect for the agility this seemingly impossible process requires is captivating. This activity always has us playfully laughing, and it is one for the memory book.

Baking Bread

"Grams, what are we going to do today?" Madi sleepily asked from her cozy cocoon of a bed she always devises in my closet when she visits. "I think I have a great idea! What do you think about learning how to make homemade bread?" I tossed out lightly. "I would love it! I have never tried it before, but it sounds amazing," my eager, adventurous 14-year-old granddaughter replied. Marvelous magic of learning and creating swirled around us as we launched our enthusiastic energy into measuring, stirring, and kneading the dough. I say "our" enthusiastic energy, but really it was all Madi, with me the grandma moving and coaching her delightfully into a new talent. "I can't believe how much I love kneading this dough! I think it is my new favorite thing to do. I love how it relaxes me. I will be making it all the time. Wait until Dad tastes this bread," Madi expounded.

Sharing Bread with a Neighbor

The next day we made a second batch and decided to take a loaf across the street to an older couple. Within a half hour, there was a knock on our door, and Angie, the neighbor let us know, with a big smile on her face, how much she and her husband loved the bread. She said they sat down and ate half a loaf with butter melting on it, along with generous portions of the huckleberry, raspberry, chokecherry jam we had also sent with the bread. It took them down memory lane from when they were young, remembering their mothers' warm-hearted baking.

Special Ingredients...a Smile Away

Encourage children to entertain the idea of adding their own special ingredients when cooking, like joy, love, and laughter. Think about when you are cooking, does your mood affect the outcome? Would a batch of cookies or a meal taste the same if they were made when one was feeling energetic and happy compared to feeling tired and crabby? I don't know, would they? I do know the person giving the baked goods or meal to others would probably feel a big difference in how they felt when they presented their final product as a gift.

Kitchen Fairy

One morning Jessie Bean came quietly and carefully to my bed at her house. She was holding something delicately. "I have a new fairy," she whispered, as not to startle her new winged friend. And, she did have a little fairy in her hands! She was a smiling, clever, and sassy looking fairy with her spunky pigtails and freckles. In her lap sat a little bowl of speckled eggs. When everyone was up, it was unanimously agreed upon, she was a kitchen fairy!

Well, we guessed that one right; she has hidden herself around their kitchen for several years now. She has taken on the reputation of adding special touches to different foods while they are cooking, and we know she is good luck. She is well loved by the whole family. She couldn't have found a more interesting and curious group in one household.

ENCHANTMENT ALERT! At times, the kitchen fairy does invite some of her fairy and elf friends to her adopted kitchen. One never knows what might happen. She and her friends might stir something up in the middle of the night and leave it with a note for the whole family.

A Picnic in the Winter

Kids love this type of activity—of going opposite to the reality of the real world. Together you can generate the menu. It makes it easier that today you can even find watermelon in the stores in the middle of winter. Make the same types of things you would include in the summer: potato salad, chicken, burgers, homemade cookies or cake, and add something sparkling or colorful to drink. Remember to ask the children about their favorite food choices. If you are having this event in the winter, and the grandkids are coming to your house, have them bring their favorite summer outfit. When they ask why, tell them it's a surprise. Fresh flowers can be a nice touch, and the picnickers may skillfully weave them into their hair for this occasion. Spread your blanket onto a comfortable spot on any floor. Kids will help come up with ideas for the occasion like moving a few plants close by to support the idea of a picnic scene. Paper plates and fun napkins are a nice touch. I have a picnic basket with dishes that works well. Summertime music in the background may be part of the event. Close your eyes and come up with what would make this come alive, and have the children add their touches. In our world, s'mores are a must. Now, if this is in the middle of the winter, it is still easy to accomplish this feat. A microwave or a gas stove work well for cooking the marshmallows. Then comes the chocolate and the graham crackers. Hello summer! This is a real time to reminisce about past and future summer pleasures. It will be fun to ask children about their memories.

There are so many opportunities to be had around cooking and eating to create fun times as well as learn important life skills. And what can be more fun than creating your own special family traditions around mealtimes?

CHAPTER 7

SAVORING MOMENTS (A MINI-CHAPTER)

S avoring something is not just for food. You can use the idea of savoring for almost any flight of fancy. You can expand this idea of savoring to time spent together. Once children learn the concept, using this one word—savor—gives them an expansive way to greet the moments in their worlds. It is a gift that lasts a lifetime. They find it an interesting challenge to be more aware and involved in sensing and appreciating. This can be an early stage of their journey to mindfulness.

Once you utter, "Let's really savor this," then it's a lot of fun to pick out special things that strike each of you. "I love the luscious smells of the flowers. The colors are exquisite! The sand feels so delightfully funny when it squishes between my toes, and it is so warm. Can I pick up a handful of it? Look at those crows. I heard some of them can talk, if trained. Can I catch one?!"

And with a nod, a wink and a smile, the scene is set at a new level. You may know crows are up for the challenge of letting young ones gets rather close. Then, with lighting speed, they lithely soar to the trees above, and with several loud caws, they seemingly invite the children into a cat and mouse game—or would that be a bird and child game?

One of the gifts available to you from the idea of savoring adventures with children is it can remind you that any event or moment like a walk in the park, sitting on a porch, a bubble bath, cooking, or just spending time with someone can take on extra special meaning if you are up for the challenge. It basically brings to mind the awe and joy in moments of connections.

(Just looking back at this thought, I have been reminding myself again and again to savor the days I get to spend writing this book.)

A little reminiscing on a hike with my husband. Earlier on in our relationship, when we would go on long hikes, I filled part of the time giving him information on how I would like to write this book at some point in time. On one hike, I was supporting my idea of how the conscious mind can come up with ideas and the unconscious mind can feel like it really happened if the picture is clear enough using senses and feelings. As we rounded a bend in the trail, and we were coming up to the meadow where we always stopped to have lunch, I imagined, "It would be like this. Pretend there is a table for two in the meadow close to the trees on the wild green grasses. The white tablecloth is covered with an array of wildflowers in a crystal vase, the dishes are a rich, light sky blue with deeper, blue forget-me-nots around the edges. The serving pieces are highly polished silver. The tall crystal champagne glasses capture the sun's rays while turning them into reflecting rainbows of romance. I'm in a stunning teal gown with thin diamond straps trailing over my shoulders." I could go on and tell you about the meal, how it was served and the sounds we heard, plus dancing together in the forest, but I think this paints enough of the picture. Anyway, when we now round this bend in the trail, and we are going to stop for lunch, the first memory I have is this remarkable time we shared together many years back. It just happens this scene pops into my memory, and still feels like it happened.

On this same hike, as I was explaining to him how the fairies and elves can be anywhere, we came to this dramatically tilting five-foot-long flat rock area that had water tumbling over the top edges creating a perfect water slide. I envisioned a lovely and lively scene of elves and fairies sliding over this rock and down to the bottom to only jump or fly back up to the top for another exhilarating ride. Again, to this day, as we walk by this rock, the fondness of this scene generates pleasing smiles in my heart as it all comes to life. I must say for a brief second, I find myself looking around expectantly in hopes of catching one of these elusive characters.

CHAPTER 8

GIVING AND RECEIVING

THE IDEA OF GIVING

Writing a note, leaving a flower, or leaving a treat for the elves and fairies will make children's hearts smile. The act of giving to others while recognizing the other's joy in receiving is a pleasure that once learned lasts a lifetime. And that pleasure grows to huge proportions when the idea of giving freely without expecting something in return is understood, appreciated, and enjoyed.

Little fairies' wings grow and change when children find winsome ways to make heartfelt sparkles, like petting an animal, giving a hug, or saying thank you. It is a wonderful thing when children learn to give back at an early age. This ability becomes a natural part of their lives by seeing or feeling the sparkles of love and wonder that they have had a part in creating.

Being A Secret Pal or Neighborhood Elf or Fairy Helper

Once a month or so, help the child pick out someone to surprise by making them something and delivering it. The recipient may be someone in the neighborhood who is a bit lonely or perhaps just because. If you want to keep the surprise a secret, part of the adventure can be finding a time when the person or family would be less likely to see you deliver this bit of a mystery. Children really enjoy this part of the adventure. This gift can be anything from a hand-drawn picture, a note, flowers, or something you baked. I wouldn't encourage things like a brand-new adorable puppy or a ridiculously cute kitten no matter what kind of a basket it would be delivered in. A goldfish would still be a little over the top. One of the best parts of secret giving is learning to keep the secret. It's very hard for little ones to do but well worth the effort. And it makes for great fun between the secret keepers since they know that they are the only ones who know who is really making and delivering those special gifts.

A Mystery Gift

This next recounting is an amazing example of a mystery gift. It happened to my mom. She needed a new recliner. Hers was at the point that I think someone was afraid one of the small grandchildren might get lost in the sagging cushion. One day, a delivery truck pulled up in front of her house, and there was a perfect new chair for her. Mom told them she hadn't ordered it. They insisted on leaving it with her. They told her it was paid in full. It took her a couple of days before she sat in it; she thought they would realize their delivery mistake and be back to claim it. She kept looking at the receipt and the reading the "PAID IN FULL" stamped on it. She ended up loving the chair. But one of the biggest sources of curiosity and joy in this situation was no one ever admitted to sending her the chair. She asked many a person in her life more than once, but no one even cracked a secretive smile. You could hear her saying, at times, "I'm always up for a good mystery, but this one really has me stumped!" To this day, the only person who knows the truth is the playful, giving person who sent the chair.

Presents from the Elves and Fairies

ENCHANTMENT ALERT! Elves and fairies can bring random little presents, notes, or little confections that might be tucked under a bed or pillow, or in a small mailbox in the child's room. They will often leave a note that lets you know a treasure hunt is needed to find the present. Kids love this type of a little adventure in the morning. The grandkids tell me the fairies and elves leave them presents more often when we are all together. I guess these wee characters know that we are anticipating their visits.

Entry into Imagination

Another place to leave notes and give and get little presents could be by a little door attached to a tree or any place in a yard or in the house. The door could be about four or six inches high. You can have a lot of fun making the door out of sticks and leaves and pine cones you find around the yard. Or, if you have someone who is handy with working with wood, a custom door can be made that leads into the realm of the fairies and elves. Use your imagination and use the imagination of others by reading illustrated books on the wee folk and searching the internet for other ideas.

A Repair Station

ENCHANTMENT ALERT! Jessie Bean has a shelf in her bedroom where she has most of her fairies. She will put whatever is broken on the shelf, and with a big smile, simply states, "Don't worry, Grandma. I put broken things on my shelf with my fairies, and they fix it. It may take a couple of days, but they always fix it." Ah, the gift of the wee ones to repair broken objects!

Sparkle Boards

Fairies and elves have what they call sparkle boards. They are a bit like a journal. They add to them when they have run into sparkles or helped others to sparkle. These "others" can include humans or animals. You might find them getting a baby bird to safety when it couldn't find its way home. You get many sparkles that way; the bird's family find their hearts sparkling as does the baby bird's. They can add to their sparkle boards when they complete a task. One of the great values about these boards is they are just for themselves—no competition or anyone checking on them. They can add sparkles when they have a feeling they have handled a situation to the best of their ability. Their favorite sparkles are when they help bring to others smiles, laughter, and hearts that shine a little brighter.

With encouragement from the adults in their worlds, children can learn to understand how other people's hearts may smile more when the child spends a little time with them. Giving small gifts like a hand-drawn picture, a favorite flower, or one of their creative hand-painted rocks lets the child share a bit of themselves while creating lots of sparkles in themselves as well as in the people or characters receiving the presents.

GIVING THE GIFT OF TIME AND IMAGINATION

The gift of time and imagination can be the most precious gift one can give. And all you need is a willing heart! Being truly present is a wonderful skill for children to learn. It is also a skill that many of us could use a refresher course on! Our busy lives sometimes make us feel like the last thing we want to do is sit down and really be with someone who is not already a good friend. How do we give of ourselves in an easy, relaxed yet fun way? Here are some suggestions:

Imagining Scenes with Other Grown-Ups or Children

In my work with some of my elderly, homebound clients, I would go on imaginary trips with them. Their concerns would float away: their bodies worked beautifully, they felt like they were pain free for a few moments, they became agile, and they could afford anything their hearts desired. We would keep our eyes closed and pick a place we wanted to explore. This might find us at the beach as the sun was beginning to dip its shining edges into the welcoming ocean all while the waves sang their rhythmic majestic beats. Sitting youthfully and expectantly at a table for two, you would find us smartly dressed for the occasion in elegant attire, with jewels and shoes that lived up to the occasion. The table would be covered with a white tablecloth adorned with fragrant tropical flowers. As the distinguished waiters returned for orders, we knew no limits. Dancing champagne bubbles filled the elaborately-designed chilled glasses. We picked each course and savored every bite while talking about the pleasure of spending time together on this trip. We enjoyed relishing in all the sights and sounds, including the serenading music. The evening might find us slipping off our shoes and walking in the still-warm sand from the setting sun. On some of the trips, we would giggle when a gallant, handsome man would approach our table and ask my client to dance. This would find them twirling in the night air with radiant smiles and slightly blushing cheeks. Such freedom and joy! All of this might end with us sitting on the beach finding seashells and running our fingers through the sand. Oh, I forgot the dessert! These were always ornate creations that seemed to be sent from heaven. The one consistent thread in these confections were they always had some sort of chocolate involved in the magic. I can see you might be wishing you had gone on some of these trips with us.

Spending Time in a Nursing Home

If you don't know a resident in a nursing or assisted-living home, you can call a social worker at a facility to see if there is someone who would enjoy a visit from a child. There are a number of people in these facilities who don't have visitors. It is a great way to see the joy materialize for both the child, the recipient, and probably yourself. The gift of time, making a drawing, giving a note, or making a small confection are a few ways to have fun with this visit while teaching children about giving and enjoying others. Initially, I advise keeping the visits short; children can get bored. You may find someone who likes games, storytelling (or going on imaginary trips!), drawing, or singing songs.

Games

Keeping a deck of cards, a travel Scrabble, or chess board means that you are always ready to have fun. And while you are at it, throw in a pack of markers and a drawing pad. There will be tools enough to inspire everyone to express themselves in creative enjoyable moments. Oh, and what about Mad Libs? Who doesn't like creating silly stories out of random words? Sometimes the easiest way to be present with others is through a shared activity.

A Gift of Time: A Story of Mom and Dad

Every week, my mom and dad had been visiting my mom's cousin in the nursing home. On one of these visits, my mom noticed that she recognized the name on one of the other resident's door, Mrs. Beverly Wakely. Mrs. Wakely had lived across the street from my grandparents' home when mom was young. Mom spent a great deal of time with Mrs. Wakely's children.

Well, Mom and Dad popped in to visit her that day, and those visits continued for the next three years. They would bring her different simple presents like flowers from the garden and little delicious treats. They had the best of time with my mom entertaining all three of them with stories from childhood memories in the old neighborhood. Mom would tell her how much she appreciated the things Mrs. Wakely would do like baking cookies and coming up with fun activities for all. Mom said Mrs. Wakely would smile a great deal, and say things like: "We had a good time, didn't we? I just can't remember it." Or, "What a lovely story, I wish I could remember those times." Or "I always look forward to you coming to visit. It brings me such pleasure."

Anyway, one day my dad was reading the paper and there was Mrs. Wakely's obituary; she had passed away that week. He read the obituary out loud to my mother. The more he read, the more perplexed Mom became. "Wait a minute," she said, "I always thought she was from Kansas, not Florida. She only had three kids I knew about, not five! No, those aren't the names of her kids."

As you might be guessing by now, the Mrs. Wakely who they had been visiting was not the one Mom had known when she was growing up some 50 years earlier.

When I think of this story, I chuckle some, but then I think about the wonderful times this Mrs. Wakely had during her last years with these weekly visits with my mom and her full heart and my dad with his sense of humor and kindness. I can't forget the bonus of all the stories Mrs. Wakely heard, she enjoyed, and felt she had been a part of in earlier years. Mom and Dad were a rare and consistent gift for Mrs. Wakely. Well, other than Mrs. Wakely wishing she had more of a memory for those fun story-filled years.

Over the Garden Gate

When my mom passed, we received a note from a person who had grown up in our neighborhood. He wrote, "I wanted you to know how much I have always appreciated your mother. When I was young, I didn't really have anyone who spent time with me, but when I would walk by your mother's garden, she would always stop what she was doing and spend all of her time just talking to me, for it seemed, as long as I wanted or needed. She would ask me questions about myself, and I felt someone cared about me. I don't know if she ever realized how much all of those visits meant to me." A reminder of the importance of how significant a smile, compliment, or the gift of undivided time and positive attention may mean to others in our lives.

CHAPTER 9

EXPLORING THE MYSTERY AND ENCHANTMENT IN AND WITH THE GREAT OUTDOORS

Let the fun of exploring begin in yards, gardens, at beaches, in forests, and in deserts where radiant and plentiful plants and flowers dance into existence in spring and summer and fade into fall and winter. Adjust for your own environment's beautiful rhythms. Mix in diverse groups of animals, birds, insects, and water life and the palette of interests increase. Then sprinkle in the lively lore of the fairies and elves, (ENCHANTMENT ALERT!) magnifying enchantments by way of your imagination.

Gathering Ice Crystals in Winter

You already know the fairies can gather ice crystals for their wings, but you may not know that both the fairies and elves gather them in special containers to be used throughout the seasons. One of the tricks they use to find the most spectacular crystals is they squint their eyes and the elaborate designs of the crystals will heighten to the grandeur of rainbows themselves. Try this yourself—on a sunny day, when the ice crystals are beaming and glittering in all their uniqueness, squint your eyes and watch as the crystals start emanating spokes of rainbow-infused light. Then you will know that you have experienced the hidden amplifications of crystalline grandeur.

Ice Castles and Frozen Puddles

If you are fortunate enough to find a place with thick ice on a frozen puddle with some openings in the top, try peering into this wonderland of possibilities. It can truly look like a fairy's ice castle. Noticing the rare display of astonishing beauty can quietly lift one's spirit. I explored these types of crystal palaces as a child. With memories of these adventures filling my mind and heart, you can still find me, when the opportunity arises, on my stomach on the ice while looking into a bit of truly remarkable elegance.

Clues in the Snow of the Wee People's Playfulness

If you are walking in the snow on a trail or up a hill, start looking around. If you discover tiny clumps of snow, you can be pretty sure the wee ones were trying their skills at making snowballs while displaying their agility in dodging these tufts of snow. Picture the wee ones during their snowball fights. Consider how the fairies' ability to fly and the elves' ability to jump high or low in a split second affects the game. Their one rule is they can't just use their magic and disappear. Well, unless a human is approaching!

Usage of Crystal Dust in the Springtime

Come springtime, the elves and fairies put some of their crystal dust on their feet, and they carefully walk around some of their favorite springtime plants to waken them from their winter's interlude of rest. These wee characters love using the crystal dust as a gentle reminder of the approaching season. These plants would pop up anyway, but it is nice to be welcomed back by their special friends. There is much celebrating in the spring as life begins to robustly emerge. Beauty, love, and exquisite enchantment seems to touch all of our hearts with the approaching season of spring. If we stop and take time to savor these moments, the gifts of nature will be plentiful and enhance the quality of our moments.

Exploring Nature with Walks and Hikes

Because of the possibility of the elves or fairies being close by, my granddaughters Olivia, Madi, and Jessie Bean and my grandson Greyson never turn down hikes. Rounding a bend in a trail, we are always anticipating the idea of a bustling elf

and fairy village disappearing the instant before we arrive. We scan the scenes closely as we pass by for clues. Or one of the grandchildren will accept the challenge to climb up steep rocky inclines to search for evidence of wee characters. Our anticipating hearts expect to discover some of these tantalizing artifacts: from interesting rocks to other objects like bottle tops, nut shells, moss, pine cones, or curled leaves. We talk about what the fairies and elves might use them for: dishes, furniture, traps, and decorations. Tiny pools of water with flowers and berries around them may be places for them to swim, play, and catch rainbows. Trees with one or more holes in their trunks might be a condominium of treasures bursting with magical energy. We always wish we could see inside of them. We also inspect the trunk of trees for holes that are probably doorways. When we see or hear small animals who are touted to be friends with the fairies and elves, we know this means there is a good chance the wee ones are close by. When we see a particularly noisy squirrel, we figure it has a fairy or elf comfortably riding on its back. Different noises in the forest oftentimes have us wide-

eyed and guessing how the wee characters might have created this or that noise. Leaves, twigs, or feathers floating, swirling, and diving down a stream totally catch our attention while our imaginative minds form the pictures of our dreams. What about little dust storms being stirred up by the fairies using their wands to send a proper "hello"? I don't think any of us have ever felt our bountiful experiences lacked anything; we saw enough shadows and fast movements to have us fully captivated and ready for the next adventure in the woods. Please remember we have the woods as part of our lives, but you don't need to live near a forest. Most all of these same experiences can happen in parks, zoos, backyards, in the city, and truly all different terrains. One of my friends, who grew up in densely populated Brooklyn, New York, vividly remembers her walks to school each morning with her dad. She passed dozens and dozens of postage stamp-sized gardens walking the city streets hand in hand with her father. She had her favorite places to look for magical characters hiding behind rose bushes or under leaf piles.

If walks or hiking are the adventure, start out with short distances, and have the time spent full of intrigue. If children remember being tired, bored, or they feel like they have to do it, you may meet with resistance. On the other hand, if they are fully and pleasantly engaged both consciously and unconsciously, they may well be hooked on this and it becomes one of their favorite activities. I would say that is an excellent gift that can last a lifetime.

I find that when small children are focused on exploring their environments in playful ways which capture their curiosity, investigative and imaginative skills, plus encourage budding interests, they can't help but fall in love with the adventures.

BEING A NATURE DETECTIVE

Nature has many interesting gifts of flora and fauna to choose from for beginning, young, curious detectives. There is both an art and a science to being a full-fledged nature detective!

Trees

Let's say you start with trees. There are many things to discover about the different varieties of trees. It's great to start, like a good detective would, by asking lots of questions. Here are a few to start with. You, I am sure, will come up with more:

How do they smell? Do they need lots of water or just a little? Do they produce fruit? What do their leaves look like? Do they lose their leaves in the winter or do they keep them? If they lose their leaves, what color do those leaves turn before they fall? What kind of bark do they have? What do their branches look like if you lie on the ground and look up at them? What are their uses for humans or for other creatures?

Using the trained eye, plus knowledge, match fallen leaves to the various trees in your yard, neighborhood, in parks, or in the woods while walking through on one of the long days of summer or in one of the fall days of brilliance. You can dry these leaves in a book to start a collection. It's easy: carefully lay them between two of the pages of a book, and close it gently around them. You can make cards with pictures and information on them. Have the

children draw the pictures. These cards can turn into a memory game of information gathered and a nice way of reminiscing about earlier jointly shared adventures.

You can take any other part of nature and do your detecting. Flowers, insects, small animals, clouds, etc., are all there waiting to be seen and understood. Each child will have their preferences as to which aspects of the natural world capture their attention. Becoming a nature detective means that you will never run out of things to discover. You don't really need to prepare for nature detecting, it can happen any time, day or night, winter or summer, rain or shine; there are always things to explore!

Another way to approach nature detective work is to take a specific place— your backyard or a portion of a nearby park or even a special place in the forest or the beach—and decide you will really notice everything about the place. This can be a great ongoing fun activity with a child as you get to discover how the place changes or stays the same throughout the day, the seasons, and from year to year.

Friends of the Animals

Fairies and elves consider animals their best friends. This includes household pets like cats and dogs. But it also includes the rest, so when you see creatures of the forest, zoo, or in some fields like a rabbit, a little deer, even a skunk, there could be an elf or fairy sitting on its back or lazily reclined on its soft fur.

You may be thinking, "Skunks?! Really?" Well, actually, skunks get a bad reputation because they instinctively protect themselves with a scent that is quite powerful and lasts an extremely long time! People, like fragrance chemists, or as I call them, "perfume magicians," are quite in awe of the skunk's ability to so easily and consistently produce a product that most everyone, maybe in the whole world, knows by smell or, at least, by name. And, you must admit, high-end perfume companies would love to have the same level of recognition for their products.

By the way, skunks never spray the elves and fairies. When the elves and fairies are sitting around visiting with the skunks, the skunks love to regale them with many a story of their interesting encounters. There is many a hilarious story about how they hide until they think a human or dog is going to wander within range. They think it's quizzical when a dog runs straight up to them, often-times growling and baring their teeth. And, with one little spray, they are yelping and running to their humans and then whining and rolling in the dirt. The skunks start laughing so hard they turn into black and white balls of comedy. They actually look like miniature tuxedos.

Well, you can imagine the stories the skunks tell about the owners of these dogs when they are greeted with this terrifically strong, recognizable scent. A few of the owners start yelling and running from the dog, which gives the dog the impression they have been invited to a good game of catch and jump on the owner.

Another scenario, which is just as funny in the skunks' opinion, is when the owner tries to get the dog in a creek, if there is one. The skunks love to take a hidden, ring-side seat to watch the owner trying to drag the dog into the water with the dog going stiff-legged and pushing back with all of its might. The owner is yelling, and the dog wants to growl, but the terror of what's happened and what's to come has it dazed like it's in a dream. Once they hit the water, the real fun begins—from the skunks' perspective. The dog tries jumping out. The owner ultimately has to get the dog in a bear hug, and then tries to scrub the smell out with his or her bare hands. The ridiculous part, the skunks feel, is the owners don't realize until coming out of the churned up, muddy water that they didn't really wash any of the smell off of the dog. Surprisingly, they ended up smelling just like the dog! The skunks always stay for the grand finale when the dog starts vigorously shaking water and the scent into an already hilarious scene.

Telling stories of this sort about animals can be a good way to add information about how to deal with particular animals, what they are like, and if they are friendly or not. And even if an animal is small or seems docile, children should be educated about all wild animals and the wisdom of always giving them lots of space so as not to disturb them in their natural activities and patterns. Once children have increased knowledge about and respect for different animals, they can make up stories that take the point of view of the animal and its unique way it looks at the world and situations. The possibilities are endless once you start telling stories like this. And children love to imagine what it is like to really be a particular animal. Don't be surprised to find out that the child in your life feels a special affinity to one kind of animal. It's always interesting to notice what a child is drawn to.

Elves and Fairies and their Beloved Birds

When a bird is flying close by, one of the wee people could be catching a ride on its back. As they pass by, I imagine them waving and smiling with a greeting. This is a good time for learning about different types of birds. If a young child is lucky enough to have a companion who happens to be a "birder," or a bird enthusiast or aficionado, then the teaching can innocently begin. By the time they are five, children may have a great respect and knowledge of the birds they encounter. It wouldn't seem so much like learning but just a way to start to recognize which of the birds might be best friends with the elves and fairies. This knowledge can become a family game of recognizing the bird, its song, and some details about it. It never hurts to have a bird book close at hand for the extra details, if you care to take it further. Look out for bird identification books specific to your region or environment.

A Game of Pretending

A fun game is to pretend that you jump up on the branch with a bird. What does the bird look like close up? What would it be like to look down from the branch? What would it feel like to be sitting on the branch? Listen intently—what different sounds might you hear? What would it feel like to fly away? You can create this game with birds, animals, flowers, trees, or anything in children's environments like rocks, furniture, foods, or books, to mention a few. More questions you could include: What would a tree in wind experience? What does the tree experience when an animal lightly runs across its branches? What it is like having a squirrel living in its trunk and filling it with treasures? When someone attaches a swing to its stronger branches and children come to laugh and play around the tree, does it like this activity, or it is a disturbance? Do trees talk to the other trees? What might a tree be sensing or feeling? There are so many investigative journeys of imagination to be explored. I think adults will thoroughly enjoy these journeys as well as the children.

This type of exploration really creates an interactive way of learning to see one's environment in detail and with great appreciation. Rather than the child thinking how they themselves would think and feel, they are trying to go outside of themselves to look at bigger worlds. This type of play supports growing imaginations and the ability to brainstorm, which I believe are excellent tools in supporting oneself in creating a rich and full life. Later on in the book, I give examples of how adults can employ different ways of engaging with music. The same philosophy is behind both.

A Memorable Backpacking Trip: The Dad, The Five-Year-Old Child, and an Unwelcome Mystery Guest

Madi remembers a story from the great outdoors when she was five years old and on a backpacking trip with her Dad. She says, "I was sitting on a log with my dad by our campfire. We were on one of our famous backpack trips and ended up setting

up our campsite away from our targeted camping spot. This was
mainly because we never found that spot and it was starting
to get dark. This happens with my dad from time to time. After
setting up our tent and having dinner, we were relaxing on a log
by the fire, drinking hot chocolate with little marshmallows and
telling stories. As I looked into the deep dark forest, I thought I
could see some of the fairies and elves, and I could really hear
them moving around. I knew the happiness of our home away
from home would seem magical to them. You see, I know a lot
about fairies and elves. Anyway, I was staring so intently into the
forest, I was the first one to spot this very large creature, and not
only did I spot him, but I yelled in a high-pitched scream to my
dad, 'Is that an elk or a moose running towards us?' With that
hardly out of my mouth, I dove for the little opening in the tent.
I was so scared, and I was shaking so bad, the whole tent was
shaking. My dad tells his story, like this. 'When Madi yelled, and
I looked up, there was a big bull moose charging us. I don't know
why I had my bear spray sitting right next to me, but I responded
within seconds. The amazing thing was the moose kept charging

until it was about two feet from me. I was sure it wasn't going to stop. It was phenomenal to get a glimpse of Madi diving into the tent when the zipper was only open about seven or eight inches. The only thing sticking out were her feet.'" Madi finishes, "My dad did great, but I was a little concerned because afterwards, he started giving me some words of wisdom. He started telling me if anything like this should happen, again, and I was left by myself, I needed to head to the car which would be down the hill. Well, you can imagine my concern, we were out in the woods, and we had never found the real campground in the first place. I felt I was a little young for this type of information. Oh, I want to tell you the rest of the story, my version, of stopping the moose. Certainly, the bear spray helped. But I think what happened, was a couple of the elves jumped into the moose's nose, and the fairies and other elves jumped on those huge antlers and started pulling him backwards. Now, you can imagine the whole scene. And, yes, my dad and I have been on many more camping trips, and now we take my little sister, Jessie Bean. Plus, my dad always has his bear spray strapped to his chest at all times."

CHAPTER 10

CREATING MAGICAL ENVIRONMENTS

Fairy Houses

Creating fairy and elf stopping places like decorated birdhouses or building the houses from scratch with an adult can add up to an entertaining—and productive—time spent together. These activities can teach many skills in terms of planning, gathering, and building one-of-a kind creations. The best part, however, is the time you have spent together and the memories you have constructed out of thin air.

When Madi was seven years old, and her cousin Olivia was five-and-a-half, we did a project like this. Both of their moms helped with gathering materials and helped them follow through with their unique designs for these charming creations. Yes, I was included in this adventure. The beginnings of these houses were made out of gazebo-type bird feeders. Adding an ample supply of ribbons, pearl strands, rhinestones, grasses, twigs, and little garlands of flowers and plants gave them just the right touches. These fairy houses started taking on personality within several hours. I happily warn you, though, that these types of productions can lead to building furniture or other items out of twigs, rocks, feathers. It's also perfectly fine to get supplies from your house, garage, or local stores—you don't have to solely rely on found objects outside. And you can structure a project like this anywhere. If you are in the garden, in a park, or in the woods, make the house out of mud, sticks, rocks, and leaves. Children can come up with many inventive ideas for these types of inspirational projects. Mom and dads can pass on a number of building tips if they build a house from scratch with their child. A big bonus for you, as the adult, is you are working right alongside them with your ideas, ability, and enthusiasm. You can imagine how special this type of time spent together will mean to you both.

After a number of years, Madi passed her intricate fairy house on to her little sister, Jessie Bean. It is still an exceptionally loved creation in their home.

If you think you need some ideas for these kinds of habitats, I would first encourage you to let your child dream up some plans. If you still would like more ideas, look at a few books you may have with fairy stories or take a trip to the library to find some beautiful picture books. This can be a part of the adventure of building your fairy house. And then, of course, there is always the internet for seeing how others envision these charming abodes. I believe you will find that you will have as much fun with this project as the children.

Jessie and I constructed a fairy and elf house in 2019. Most of our building materials came from contractors who were building in our neighborhood. When we let them know about our project, they would smile and direct us to the leftover building materials where we gratefully found items to help create our vision.

Add A Plant or Flower to a Room

You can have a child pick out a plant or flower to care for which will live in their room. An added bonus is this can be an invitation to establish a place where fairies and elves may stop by. Children will have fun planning how to organize this space. It can be as simple as adding a few of their treasured rocks (maybe painted by the child) or drawing pictures to set next to the plant so the wee characters know they are welcome. They may like leaving them other notes or adding shiny or colorful treasures of interest that will draw the curiosity of fairies and elves.

Stemming from the initial choice of the plant, children can learn how it will best thrive. Does it need light or is it better in the shade? How often does it need water and how much? What about fertilizer? This easily teaches them how to explore beyond the first excitement of getting the plant to learning about responsibility and the importance of ongoing care. If the plant doesn't thrive, hopefully you give the child a big hug, and say something like, "That's life, and we will try again."

Fairy Garden Trays

Creating a little fairy garden on a tray to keep indoors where the fairies and elves can come and listen when someone is practicing an instrument, reading, or studying is a source of support and happiness for children and the fairies and the elves. These trays may include sand, shiny objects, and anything which catches a child's eye and the fairies' and elves' interest.

A Nook in Your Home

You can set up a special place to receive and send notes, presents, and visits. In our bonus room in our house, we have an open closet-type area that I turned into a calming and charming fairy and elf world with each of the walls and ceilings painted different colors which happen to match a colorful chandelier. The chandelier is on a dimmer switch which allows us to create different moods. At its brightest setting, it allows us plenty of light to curl up together to read or talk about the day's adventures. The floor is covered in a colorful, comfortable foam mattress, adorned with eight different fluffy pillows to add to our pleasure. At the entry, there are a set of chimes which had been at my parents' home. I'm sure my mom would agree the chimes are a perfect addition to what we call Fairy and Elf Land.

When Greyson comes to visit, the first thing he does is run up the stairs and ring the chimes to call all the elves and fairies. Then we pop into this enchanting world, and spend some time jumping into adventures in a two-by-three foot whimsical painting my husband created which depicts treehouses in a forest with children playing in water along with a number of elves and fairies. If you have a closet or small room, you may enjoy the happiness in a created area like this one above.

Creating a portal to magic realms of beauty and adventure is easy. You can use one of the suggestions above or simply take a bookshelf and grace it with special objects. Just make sure that it does not get stale! Keep it fresh with flowers and new objects from the natural world as well as those that you and the child have made. Before you know it, that enchanted bookshelf will become a beloved spot in your house!

CHAPTER 11

A CUPBOARD FULL
OF ADVENTURES

There are a lot of intriguing adventures to be had just at home. Adventures can be ready with or without props. Just jump into the fun!

ON THE HUNT FOR ELVES AND FAIRIES

ENCHANTMENT ALERT! "Oh Grandma, I just saw a fairy…or an elf!" Madi yelled. …and the chase is on. Darting from flowers to plants to rock piles, a world of exploration, entertainment, and laughter ensued, bringing us closer to our energetic and curious friends from the wee people's world.

"It's an elf. I saw his green hat. I'm after him!" And away Madi scampered, racing across the backyard with me (Grandma, of course) right behind her. Carefully and quietly peering under the big bush, we discover a few pieces of rainbow-colored paper and a beautiful blue bottle cap.

"It's amazing! Right here in our backyard." Madi's imagination jumped ahead, and she decided the blue bowl (cap) and rainbow curtains (paper) were part of the wee people's household. With an impish grin, she surmised, "I guess when they saw us coming, they didn't have time to make everything disappear. We are very fast, aren't we, Grandma? They are so cute. I'm sure I heard a little bell. Will Fred [the Elf] leave me a note tonight? He loves having us chase him and his friends. I'm going to put some little berries in their bowl that they left. They will love the surprise." Chaos, adventure, and excitement filled the air around us.

"Let's get our tea party ready, Grandma. We know they are around!" Madi explained with delighted excitement. "Can we set a spot for them? Great. I will pick some flowers to surprise the fairies and the elves when they show up. They are going to love our cookies we made this morning. I loved cracking the eggs. It's so fun adding the different colored pansies on the top of them. I had a great idea, didn't I?" Madi stated with satisfaction.

As the tea party ensued, we began a bit of serious detective work watching for movement from the leaves, flowers, or grasses for clues.

"Grandma, look!" Madi whispered with her finger up to her lips. "The hummingbirds are coming. I can't wait to see if the fairies are catching a ride on them. That is where I think I saw one, but she disappeared as quickly as I looked. Be very still, Grandma."

Later, the cookies we were eating disappeared at what seemed to be an impossible rate of speed as we spent the next couple of hours relaxing on our lawn chairs while reading and chatting.

"I love being at your house, Grandma. There is so much to do. I'm getting so hot, do you think we could run through the sprinklers and play on the slip-n-slide?" Madi asked happily, as she kept in mind this adventure always brings her little friends closer, they love water, sparkles, and laughter. And no one laughs more than the two of us when we are engrossed in activities in the backyard.

As the evening drew near, Madi asked me, "Grandma, can we sleep on the deck tonight? Do you think the elves and fairies will watch the stars with us? These are some of our best times, aren't they? Just you and me staying up late on the porch, playing games, while we watch the stars' twinkling faces as they pop out. Mom said spending time with someone is one of the greatest gifts you can give each other. We sure know how to do that, don't we?"

And this is how easily an afternoon drifting into evening can unfold!

Inviting Hawaii In

Hawaiian decorations showed up at our home one day for the first time when we were gone picking up our three granddaughters, Madi, Olivia, and Jessie Bean. When we arrived home, they all simultaneously burst into rapid chatter, jumping up and down, and twirling around and running to the elaborately decorated Hawaiian-themed table. "The elves and fairies did this! What a surprise. Look at these grass skirts and Hawaiian leis. This is going to be so much fun. Now we know those little characters are around. We might even catch one if we are quick."

It is now a tradition to pull out the boxes with the ever-growing number of mood-setting Hawaiian decorations. Besides children and grandchildren, we now have several adult friends over for "Hawaiian" evenings with lizards, flowers, Hawaiian music, and the vibrance of reminiscing hearts easily moving into the tranquility and romance of an evening on the islands. Usually, a number of stories fill the room on these evenings, adding to the enchantment. I especially enjoy the dinners when they happen in the winter and everyone is still willing to play along and wear their summery festive Hawaiian attire.

Fun Masks

"I get the blue one with the silver sparkles!" Olivia called out enthusiastically. Jessie Bean eagerly chimed in, "I want the red one with the feathers and gold designs." Madi with great drama carefully lifted a black one out and claimed it, "I want this black one with diamonds. This one reminds me of the mysteries of the night stars!" These are my granddaughters bargaining with each other over their favorite masks. (Ah, yes, remember when masks were just for fun—the good old days! Hopefully those days will return again.) Then they were off to find their favorite dresses and shoes of mine to complete their exceptionally stunning attire for whatever events we could cook up. I now have an exquisite collection of Mardi Gras masks. The masks have also found their way to several different adult get-togethers. One gathering, I remember fondly, is when I brought the masks out, and everyone picked one, including the men. Then I suggested we tell something about ourselves like our most embarrassing moment, our favorite memory, or something the group didn't know about that person. It turned out to be a really interesting and well-received sharing. And, at the beginning, many of them were thinking this might be the last thing they wanted to participate in.

Everyday Dress-Up

Within an hour after arriving at our house, Jessie Bean, then nine years old, generally secretly disappeared into my closet and returned sporting a pair of my high heeled shoes or boots, shoes that turned her into a rare beauty of a budding teenager. This has usually set her mom into one of those moments contemplating how such a transformation can happen with just a pair of ill-fitting shoes and a little apron. I have many a picture with this bright star, her big smile, baking, stirring, or washing dishes. And her mom sighing, and saying, "I'm not ready for this." Think of how a pair of shoes might transform you or your child in your life, and have fun digging through the closet!

Greyson's Snowboard Indoors

Shortly after arriving at Greyson's house for Thanksgiving, he grins at me and questions, "Grandma, would you pull me in the basement on my snowboard?" (His snow board was a Styrofoam one he received for his birthday in October when he turned six years old.). How could I resist the big blue eyes, the grin, and the sense of adventure in his request? We headed straight to the basement. He jumped on the board in a seated position, and I started pulling him around and around the carpeted basement floor, with him asking me to go faster and faster, with both of us laughing and being silly. At one point, he shouted in delightful glee, "Grandma, this makes me feel just like a kid, again!" Just a few minutes of "snowboarding" indoors created so much joy.

Garage Sales (aka Yard Sales) and Christmas in July

"Now, remember, we have to get up early for the garage sales in the morning! I can't wait to see what treasures we might find," Madi reminded me. And thus began the expectant hunt for new valuable gems in our lives. We never look in the paper; we just fly by the seat of our pants, as they say. Madi hollers, "There's a garage sale sign Grandma, I will get the address in your phone," and off we go to beat the other early risers. One such a day of adventures had us finding things for everyone like Jessie Bean, the little sister; Jenny, the mom; and Grandpa Jim, the one holding down the fort. At this point, I looked at Madi with a twinkle in my eye, and asked, "How about Christmas in July?"—

and away we went for an afternoon of surprises for the three mentioned above.

Jessie Bean and Jenny were expected to arrive around three in the afternoon. Our time was limited for creating a full-fledged Christmas in just a few hours. But we didn't let that sway us from our chosen course! We looked at it as an extra special challenge filled with excitement, drama, and a whirlwind of activity. When we arrived home, we took all of our bags downstairs to the wrapping room. Grandpa was out on a bike ride and wasn't aware of any of the preparations. The best part was I had a fully decorated, seven-foot-tall, slender tree in the storage room which we brought out into the family room in the basement. Next, we made some fancy miniature cheesecakes and decorated them with fruit. You might be wondering how much time we had left before the arrival of the mom and sister. Well, they showed up shortly thereafter and started helping fix dinner. I lightly said, "I need to make some fudge for a birthday party at work." I realize this wasn't exactly the truth, but I did take some to the office that week. And what is Christmas without fudge? With the extra help, I realized I had time to make gingerbread drop cookies. Getting through dinner found Madi and me a little hyper, we were so excited to surprise them. Madi nonchalantly disappeared downstairs to set the scene by turning on the Christmas tree lights and dimming the house lights. She reappeared without anyone having missed her.

Now this scene was everything we had hoped for: the tree was beautiful, there were wrapped presents for everyone, including Madi and myself, Jessie Bean had at least ten presents, and the delicious treats awaited us. The surprise was the best when we ushered the three recipients down the stairs and into the magic of the moments that followed. At first, Jessie Bean was more than confused; she couldn't figure out how we were having a spontaneous Christmas in the middle of the summer. I must say, both Madi and I simply loved the gift of giving and having it be a total surprise to all of them.

ADVENTURES WITH BOOKS

Plucking-Out from Books

Shortly after he turned two years old, Greyson easily grasped the idea of plucking things out of books. I would pick out something like a food item or pop a little animal out of the picture to pet. He is the type of child that sees lots of options in life, and he started picking out things himself, like a little bird. He would grab it quick, and deliberately pop it right into his mouth and chew it up. Then, with an exaggerated twist to his little face, he would promptly spit it out, and start laughing. This story rather sums up this beautifully ingenious child.

Jumping in a Book!

"Hold my hand, let's close our eyes, and when I count to three, we will jump into this snowy day." Holding hands and swinging our arms with each count, adding in a loud swishing sound, we pretend to jump into one of our favorite books. With this entry, my daughter Erika and I found ourselves in the midst of a snowy mountain scene with kids sledding, ice skating, and building snowmen. After experiencing some of the winter fun and a good old-fashioned snowball fight, Erika proclaimed, "Mom, I'm cold and I'm really hungry." I hugged her close and said, "Let's go into the cabin and warm up by the fireplace. How does some hot chocolate sound?" Racing to the cabin, I reach out to open the door, and my four-year-old gasps and looks up at me with real concern, "Mom, you can't go in without knocking!" I lightly smiled at her, touched her sincere face, and I pretended to knock into thin air. No answer. I imaginatively explain, "Oh, I found a note on the door. It says: Please go in and warm up. Have some hot chocolate and a piece of homemade apple pie." We sat by the nice warm fire, and soon she put her little hand in mine, and we "swished" back into our living room where we turned the page to explore our next moments of travel in another season. And to think the log cabin was a little one-inch square building in the picture; the rest was our inventive, curious imaginings. This book ended up being taped and retaped as it became our favorite "jumpin" book!

Jumping into pictures and books can lend itself to a variety of shared journeys. You can impart wisdom on some of these adventures. For example, when going across a creek in the picture and you spy some potentially slippery rocks that can become an issue, you say, "Hold my hand, these rocks are slippery." Feel one of them. (Pretend to reach for one of them.) You could jump into a book on camping and dole out bits of good ideas like putting the food high up in a tree, starting a campfire, or putting one out before you leave. Do this together. If you talk them through the steps, they will feel like they accomplished the task. Maybe you see a dog, and your little one says, "Let's run and pet it!" You say, "Oh, remember to ask its owner if it is okay, and let it sniff your hand first." Granted, many children already have this information and will guide you. This is your opportunity to let them lead. You might say, "Oh, I don't think I can get across the creek. The rocks are so slippery. They may pretend to run and get you a stick to help you balance or take your hand. You can sit on the bank of a lake or river and toss in rocks. Kids don't need the picture to be complete. They are great at going beyond what the picture shows. The sky is the limit on invented, shared adventures.

Jessie Bean and I have a book about animals in a barnyard that we reach to frequently for "jumping in." I ended up getting one for my house, and there have been times where we will get our copies and FaceTime and jump into different adventures far beyond the limits of the pages in the book.

ADVENTURES WITH LAUGHTER AND PRACTICAL JOKES

Laughter is something that is always available to us to help lighten our hearts, but strangely, us grownups sometimes forget to laugh. When was the last time you really laughed? Like, a good, hearty belly laugh? Well, it's good to be around children who haven't forgotten that laughing really is the best medicine for everything!

Spontaneous Laughing

Spontaneous laughing at odd times may be considered a tradition in my household. It's when everyone ends up belly laughing, but no one knows exactly why. This contagious merriment started with Grandma Clara's unique dry sense of humor, which was followed up with her captivating, seemingly uncontrollable laughter. This would start with us giggling along with her at first, and then we would find ourselves fully laughing, which, by the end, would have most of us red-faced, some with tears running down their faces and gasping for breath. Then we would look around to make sure no one was watching us conspicuously make fools of ourselves. I think it's a genetic thing. Although it seems now that she was ahead of her time. There are laugh therapy practices and even laugh therapy coaches to help you laugh your troubles away! Madi and Jessie carry on this tradition with the greatest of success in catching everyone in its high-spirited joy.

Creating Your Own Jokes

Spencer was with another four-year-old friend when they started telling each other made-up jokes. Their laughter was contagious, and threw me into fits of giggles with each new inspired joke. After about 20 minutes or more of this exuberance, his friend's brother asked if he could speak to me in the kitchen. With a perplexed look on his nine-year-old face, he asked me to explain the jokes to him, as he wasn't getting any of them. I patted his shoulder and said it was the secret understandings of four-year-olds, and I let him know that I didn't get them either, but I did resonate with their genuine connections and added laughter. So remember: you don't even have to understand the joke to take part in the fun, especially with smaller children.

ADVENTURES WITH COLORS

For this adventure, you can find an array of colors in a picture book, a box of crayons, or different items in your environment. For example, a flower filled garden is an excellent place to find lots of colors. If you choose crayons, simply take turns picking out interesting colors and try out your imaginations, feelings, and creativity while using the five senses, and a big dash of humor to investigate all the possibilities in the richness of a simple color. A bit of a warning, if the child is young, and that depends on the child, they may try eating the crayons to get the full effects when you aren't watching. If this is the case, don't hesitate to find foods with different colors for them to explore.

The game of exploration will develop over time. Try: "If you were this color, let's say green, how would you sound?" "If you were green, how would you feel? Happy, quiet, bouncy?" "How would green taste? Spicy, sour, tart, sweet?" "If you touched green, what would it feel like?" "What if you could smell this color green?" Initially, you can give kids words and ideas to try on. Soon, they will become vastly expressive and creative in using their expanding insights and vocabulary. Besides asking them questions, engage in the game yourself. They will learn a lot from your responses. It is great when your answers are acted out, such as wrinkling up your nose at different smells, shivering when a color makes you cold, or jumping up and down when excited. Being interactive with facial expressions, changes in voice tones, and adding playful movements into this game will have children captivated. I can already hear the laughter taking form as all involved arise to the challenges giving personalities to vibrations of light (that's what colors are, after all). Note: if this is a game of just words, most children will easily get bored, so do throw in physical movement to keep things lively.

ADVENTURES WITH MUSIC

Of course, I am sure that you enjoy music, and you may have your own creative ways to experience music with children. Perhaps you have taken children to concerts or sang along with one of the many children's musicians out there. Or perhaps you sing along with the radio or a favorite album of yours. Maybe you even play an instrument and have entertained friends and family. Who doesn't love music? No matter what genre enchants you, music has the power to transport us out of whatever moment and move us into other realms.

Do you need some ideas on how you couple sound and imagination to immerse yourself into the music and bring the child in your life along? An idea I have been totally enjoying is when I hear different types of instrumental music: piano, fiddle, symphony, etc. I've been mentally trying different ways of experiencing these varied pieces. I imagine the elements that might be present in these moments and then try different variations of experimenting with it depending on the quality and tone of the music. I have compiled some suggestions I've developed to interact with music in imaginative ways. Please note that all these adventures have the extra added benefit of really putting you in the moment. You can't fully engage with the music in the past or the future, you have to fully be where you actually are—in this moment! Here are my ways to dive into music:

MUSICAL NOTES: I imagine myself as the notes. I become the notes. I see the world through what they would be experiencing. I think, if I was a note, I would be floating out and circling around a room, in a car, in the air. What does it feel like to pop out into the air gently or intensely passing by someone's face and body? Depending on the music, the experiences vary. Are the notes carefree and happy like songbirds in the spring? Or intense notes with a compelling message of sadness, fear, loss? Or are they uplifting notes of fascination and amusement?

INSTRUMENTS: Which instrument should I be? Let's pick the saxophone. Becoming the saxophone has me feeling a strength and richness of tones springing forth to greet the world. How does it feel to have the superb, expressive sounds resonating throughout the strong core if you were this instrument? Do you have a preference as to the musician? To the music? You might imagine where the music is being played and by whom. This adventure is also a lovely way to help a child get familiar with the different types of instruments and what kinds of sounds they produce. Don't forget to move past your own body of knowledge and explore different instruments from other cultures. Who doesn't want to be an Australian didgeridoo for a few moments? Or a Balinese genggong? Or even a Norwegian langeleik? (It's fun to just say the instruments' names!)

MUSICIAN: While listening to a pianist, I imagine I become this master musician. I complete the scene by feeling the solidness of the bench, becoming one with the elegance and drama of the radiant piano, and becoming one with the keys. I notice how I feel as my hands dance expertly and rivetingly across the keyboard. Depending on the length of the piece that is playing, I can also imagine the room I'm in, the audience, and what I might be wearing.

BECOMING THE ROOM: Another way to enter the music is by becoming the room where the music is being played and watching how the event unfolds. I imagine the different places, but one of my favorites is at someone's house. What am I watching as the evening unfolds? Who are the musicians and attendees? Is the setting quaint or elaborate? Is the table elegantly dressed with fine china and beautiful crystal glasses, adding to the charm of a fanciful evening?

CREATING A SCENE TO RESONATE WITH THE MUSIC: This is one of my favorite parts of this imagination game. For this, I might imagine: becoming a snowflake, while floating and dancing to the music; dancing in a rainstorm; skating on a pond in the forest; riding a wild horse as it races through a beautiful canyon with the other horses; being the horse that is running; or being the water in a creek and viewing what it might be seeing as it passes by or how it feels racing over the tops of rocks. This morning, as I was driving, a lilting, gentle piano piece was playing. It drew me in, and I became the water going down a lazy stream. I, as the water, passed by a bear taking a drink, and I splashed some water on his sleepy face. He shook his head just a little, maybe with a slight annoyance or a nod of recognition. At certain places, I would flatten the water out to a fine mirror of reflections so the blue birds and little yellow canaries could admire themselves as they dipped and swirled while catching glimpses of themselves. I loved the parade of their free spiritedness. I was fascinated by the rainbow trout hiding in the deep pools behind rocks or under the overhangs of the riverbanks. I almost chuckled when thinking about how it feels when they jet out into the water and zip up or down stream where I just happen to be at this moment.

SOME OTHER SUGGESTED SCENES: **1**. Skating on a pond on a winter's day. **2**. Becoming a bird and experiencing its world. **3**. Tromping through the kind of mud that sticks to your feet in a field of cows. **4**. Being a season like autumn while feeling the textures and patterns, and marveling at what is transpiring. **5**. Being a high-spirited horse while racing in the fields and jumping fences, while feeling the strength of one's heart and unending energy of racing to capture the grandeur of the magnificent day as it unfolds. **6**. Being laughter and joy; moving in and out of scenes while leaving a fleeting touch of wonder in hearts touched by spontaneous emotions. It did give me a bit of a tickle to think of these emotions as the best of gifts.

A Tea Party with a Charming Fiddle Player

When Jessie Bean comes to visit, sometimes she brings her favorite fancy dress plus her fiddle. We have a friend, Juliana, who loves tea parties and truly enjoys hearing Jessie Bean serenade us. We will make little sandwiches, add touches of fruit and whatever confection finds its way to treat our palates. It is quite a production enhanced by my friend regaling us of memories of High Teas she has attended around the world. She is an expert at imparting the grandeur of these occasions including the striking hats and beautiful table and tea settings, while adding in the sophistication and character of exquisite, romantic palaces. And when the young fiddler's nimble fingers and bow fill the room with angelic, lively sounds, we all feel transported to visions our hearts receive with pure joy.

Enticing the Fairies and Elves with Lively Music

ENCHANTMENT ALERT! The fairies and elves love to surprise kids and adults by visiting when there is music of all types. If you have a special place for them to rest, they will sit and listen to you play music. Don't worry, if you don't have a special place for them, you might imagine they will be perched on the back of a couch or chair, balancing on the leaf of a plant, or resting on a doorknob, to name a few. Fairies will sometimes rest on the rhythm of their wings keeping beat with the glory of the sounds of the music.

ADVENTURES WITH WORDS

Word discovery with children can bring many moments of flat-out family fun. Kids can learn to love words by learning the meaning of a new word and trying to use it. If the whole family, babysitters, and friends participate in this adventure, it can be educational and enjoyable with lasting importance. Pick a word and use it as many times in that week as you can dream up. You may be surprised at how fast children pick up this game. It's also a good, interactive dinner activity. You will be delighted with the ingenuity of all involved. You might have your week loaded with laughter and merriment with everyone's attempts to find creative ways the words can be used. Imagine this tradition growing over the years.

A FUNNY EXAMPLE: I was talking on the phone with my daughter and Greyson, her then six-year-old. They were cuddled up on the couch as we FaceTimed. With an amusing grin, he states, "I'm going to bug my mom, and she is going to want to throttle me!" He then started giggling and used the word about three more times in this conversation. Every time he had the pleasure of using the word, he started laughing at the sound of it or maybe the way it felt in his mouth as it tumbled around when he spoke it. Pure joy mixed with a mischievous twist of flat out teasing exuded from his vibrant spirit. Erika said this is now his new favorite word, and he is using it all the time.

The "new word for the week adventure" can be made even more fun by adding some rituals around the arrival of the new word. Maybe the fairies and elves deliver a sealed envelope with the word of the week. Or maybe the word just appears on a chalkboard specially designated for keeping the word alive in everyone's mind. Maybe it gets written out in magnet letters on the fridge or in frosting on a cake or a cupcake. Or maybe part of the fun is to have a treasure hunt for the word which is hidden somewhere in the house in a special box. Let your imagination be unconstrained or be spontaneous each week. Any way you do it, word adventures are genuinely and exquisitely pleasurable encounters in family splendidness!

Here is a ready-made word and phrase list for you that can be added to and changed over time. If you are wading in the word wetlands with older children, be sure to look up the word of the week in an etymology resource. It's just divine to see the origins of words and how they have evolved throughout the centuries:

absorbing	active	amusing
appealing	appearing	arouse
askance	assume	astounding

attractive

beams

a blur

brilliance

carefree

cheerfulness

circumstance

constructed

culinary

delicious

diligence

dramatic

elaborate, elaborately

enchant, enchanting

engrossing

enthrall

exceptional

exquisite

exult

fierce

flighty

fragrance

gems

giddy

glittering

grand

guess

hilarity

humorous

impressive

awe-inspiring

beautiful

bouncy

buoyant

casually

cheery

commitment

courage

dedication

determination

discombobulated

eagerly

elegant

endurance

ensnare

euphoric

exhilarated

extravagant

fanciful

fine

folklore

free

generous-spirited

glimmer

glow

grandeur

heavenly

hint

imply

impulsive

awesome

beguile

bouquet

captivate

charm

chipper

complicated

crowd

delicacy

dignified

divine

easy

elusive

energy

entertainment

exaggerated

expressive

exuberance

fascinate

flamboyant

foolish

fresh-faced

genuine

glisten, glistening

gracefully

gripping

high-spirited

hope

imposing

infer

influence	insignificant	interest
intricacies	intriguing	involve, involved
irresponsible	jaunty	joyful
jubilant	legends	lighthearted
lively	lore	lovely
luscious	lush	luster
magnificent	majestic	manner
matter	melt-in-your-mouth	merry
mischievous	mistrustfully	moist
mouth-watering	mystic	mystique
myths	occurrence	open
ornate	outwit	patterns
perplexing	perseverance	persistence
pleasant	pleasurable	pointless
radiance	regal	relaxed
remarkable	repercussion	require
reserves	resigned	rich
ridiculous	roguish	scrumptious
sensational	serious	silly
simultaneously	skeptically	solemn
spectacular	spiritedly, spiritedness	splendid
spontaneous	spry	stamina
stunning	succulent	suggestion
superb	superficial	suspect
suspiciously	temper	tenacity
texture	thoroughly	tolerate
uncomplaining	unconstrained	unhurried
unique	unplanned	upshot
utterly	valuables	vigorous
vivacious	warm-hearted	win

wink   work of art   youthful

yummy

WHAT REALLY IS AN ADVENTURE?

Adventures are quite curious. When you think about it, everything is an adventure. From the minute we are born, we are on the grand adventure of our lives. But—here's the thing—because it is our life, we may take it for granted and think that what we do is no big deal. But by thinking about how we spend our time as an "adventure," we are actually giving that time the honor and respect that it richly deserves. And don't we all deserve a truly magnificent adventure in every moment?

CHAPTER 12

TREASURED TRADITIONS

How do traditions get started? What do they mean to children and families? How do they change our relationships with ourselves and others? Do traditions need to be elaborate like a big holiday? Is there room for only a few traditions? Do you have your own family list of traditions? Can the smallest of shared, repeated events be worthy of the title "tradition" and deserve to make the list? The grandkids and I have decided that the more traditions the merrier! For us, the sense of belonging, safety, anticipation, and sharing with each other are the delicious outcome of our treasured traditions.

Here I will share a few special traditions that I have with my grandchildren. Enjoy our traditions while you think about your own and new ones to be created.

Birthday Cupcake Surprise

Where do traditions come from, how much thought goes into them, who gets to participate? Well, those are good questions. Some are spur of the moment, like the belly laughter created by the comical cupcake escapade. It all started when my friend Jen and I were lucky enough to have Jessie Bean in our world for her eighth birthday. We started the day by going to a trampoline park, then on to enjoy Mexican food, and our last stop was a visit to the cupcake bakery to celebrate. At the bakery, it took us each a few minutes of contemplation before making our choices. The case was filled with about every kind of mouthwatering cupcake you can imagine. At this point, I thought we were all enjoying our cupcakes, until I glanced at Jessie Bean. She was mostly toying with her cupcake because she was stuffed from lunch earlier. She instantly looked up at me and said, "I just feel like sticking my face in this cupcake." To which I instantly replied, without skipping a beat, "Then, why don't you?" Her head popped up with a look of shock. She questioned, "Really?" Jen smiled, and brightly stated, "I will hold your hair." And in the next instant, with frosting dripping from her nose, pleasantly blushing cheeks, and satisfied giggles, we all descend into uncontrollable laughter until our sides hurt. Not only is this considered a well-deserved tradition on Jessie Bean's birthday, it is also part of the tradition on Jen's birthday when the three of us are together. You might be asking if I participate in these amusingly, free-spirited events? Certainly—I get their favorite cupcakes and take the videos. I'm sure I would participate, but there are now only two cupcakes at these events. Hmmm. Well, everyone, including this lively pair, get a piece of a mouthwatering birthday cake after their noses are fully covered in frosting from the cupcakes.

I like the idea of discovering or creating different ways to celebrate special days, events, or holidays. Children enjoy brainstorming and adding their specialness to these unfoldings. Be open to their imaginings. These ideas can be simple, such as, starting out with a "family hug" in the morning on holidays. The grandchildren and I have our lists that we consider traditions.

Slumber Party

Grandkids always sleep wherever Grandma is sleeping. It is a slumber party in the making that we all look forward to as nightfall edges its way into our busy days. We don't want to lose a minute of time we have to spend together.

Gingerbread Houses

Decorating gingerbread houses with Grandma for the Christmas season is a long-standing tradition. Finally, the day arrives for the artistry of the grand-children's finely-honed skills of creativity to begin. To set the scene, imagine the house is filled with whiffs of peppermint, gingerbread, mint, Red Hots, M & M's, and the tantalizing smells of any other treats that grace the table for this particular event. Traditionally, this adventure begins between the day after Thanksgiving up to the week before Christmas. The bursts of laughter, anticipation, and frenzied dividing up of the arsenal of resources—candy, marshmallows, coconut flakes, and frosting—turns just as intently into the quietness of concentration and perfection as the houses magically come to life with the grandchildren's intricate and individual designs. This is as true for the five-year-old up to the 16-year-old. No one ever misses this event, and it stays in our memories as the works of art are on display for about a month in selected places in each home. I might add they are placed just out of the reach of the children's desire for just one more taste of their creation. You see, when they are decorating the houses, they do get to sample their arsenal of decorations, which is, generally, the only time during the year they get more than a few pieces of candy at one time. Who can argue with tradition?

Professional Pedicures

Going out for pedicures is a lovely way of sharing time while feeling quite pampered. Talk about savoring an event! This may happen once a year with the girls for their birthday or a summer treat. We all feel special at these moments in time and have our gorgeous nails as reminders of time spent together.

Madi, Jessie, and Greyson at the Fairy and Wizards Festival

This was an event at Tizer Botanical Gardens located in the mountains at Jefferson City, Montana. "Where are my wings? I'm not sure which ones I will wear this year!" Jessie exploded as she came dashing to the table in the kitchen for breakfast. She continued in charming exuberance, "Madi, will you fix my hair? When are we leaving?" We all gathered the necessary transformational objects to design our fascinating disguises for when we would enter this world of the other fairies, elves, and wizards who are also all decked out in their fine regalia for this annual event. The last time we went, Jenny (their mom) and I stopped to pick up Greyson. He was three-and-a-half then, and he wasn't sure what we were doing, but he was up for jumping directly into the wee people's world of fantasy and celebration.

One of the favorites of the day was the live music which ignited our dancing spirits. To see the fairy wings and shimmering outfits of imagination twirling and swaying to this captivating music was pure delight in motion. Festivals like the one we attended, including events like Renaissance festivals, can be a fabulous yearly tradition for you and the children in your life.

Crossword Puzzles

A well-honed tradition with Grandpa Jim and Jessie Bean started when Grandpa Jim asked her, at age seven, what she thought a word would be for a crossword puzzle from the New York Times. They were immediately hooked on this being one of their traditions. During the evening, Grandpa Jim starts asking, "What is a five-letter word for ___?" and the evening ritual begins. The minute she sees him go to his room and open his cell phone, she jumps in right next to him and the delight of the evening challenge unfolds. It is anyone's guess if the crossword puzzle is the most important part of this exchange or if is it simply the time they spend together.

Grandparents' Gifts

Come rain, shine, snow or sleet, the surprises must go on!
You are probably thinking, at this point, I may be relaying a story
about a postman. But who might be a person more committed
than a postman, well, you may have guessed, it's a grandparent.
A couple of our friends, Juliana and Tom, lived next door to their
son and his family. On holidays, birthdays and just because,
they would sneak over in the dark hoping any curious, peering
eyes would be covered by the heavy lids of a robust day of
enthusiastic adventures. As quiet as secret agents, they would go
about decorating and leaving notes and presents on the bushes
and trees outside of the grandchildren's bedroom windows. I get
a chuckle when thinking about all the clandestine planning and
perfect timing that went into these surprises from their beautiful
hearts.

The Art of Warmth and Surprises: May Day Baskets

The enjoyable flurry of baking yummy treats, gathering
candies, crafting little May Day baskets, finding flowers, writing
notes and drawing little pictures, and finally watching Erika's
little fingers assembling these artful surprises to be delivered to
neighbors and friends all secretively began the two days before
May Day (May 1st). She would say, "Mom, I'm so excited that
butterflies are in my stomach! Make sure you get me up early
so we don't get caught leaving the baskets. Remember, we don't
want anyone to know where they came from." The next morning,
found me—the mom—quietly heading to Erika's bedroom. As I
leaned down to carefully wake her, she threw her excited little
arms around me, gave me a big kiss on my cheek and said, "I
don't think I've slept all night. I'm so excited. Who do we get to
leave a surprise for first?" The bountiful, brilliant baskets seemed
to magically fly out of our hands as they landed on sleepy
doorsteps. We were smart about these deliveries; if we suspected
they had a ravenous, curious dog that might be looming around
a rather dark corner, we left the baskets in the mailbox with a

note on their door. These types of dogs would usually disguise their real purpose by coming up to greet us with big kisses and a wagging tail. But we knew the minute they had their playful pats and hugs and we were scurrying onto the next house that the baskets would be theirs! It's good to learn at a young age to not be tricked. Talking about being able to surprise someone and not let them know it was you, it went like this: Erika questioned, "What if someone asks us if we delivered the baskets? What do we tell them because it is a surprise? What if I start smiling?" As we brainstormed this dilemma, we decided to say, "We have a basket at our house, also." So, if we get silly grins on our faces, it will look like we are tickled to be blessed with one, too. Which was totally the truth. Erika and I delighted in this tradition for three years when she was, five, six and seven.

A Coming of Age Celebration

This is not a tradition, in that it only happened once in my home, but I include it here because it can easily be adopted as a new tradition in your home. When my daughter Erika had graduated from eighth grade and was going into high school, I thought it would be lovely for her to be honored and supported by my friends and family. She was totally surprised when she walked into the house and found a number of my friends smiling at her. I said it was a party to celebrate her. She had no idea what to say but graciously sat down in the chair reserved for her with a shyly smiling face. I'm sure some of her thoughts were, "How could my mom do this to me! What am I supposed to say? I've never heard of this type of a 'coming of age' party. I think my mom came up with this one all on her own." Of course, many religions and cultures have coming of age ceremonies—but she was not aware of them. I'm sure the fight or flight urge popped into her brain with an overwhelming urgency to depart.

My request to my friends was for them to write down their memories of her as they watched her grow over time. Almost all of them had known her since she was a baby. Besides memories, I asked them to impart some life wisdom as she was about to embark on the journey into the flamboyant and turbulent halls of high school. Besides my friends, I asked special men in her life to write something to her, and these expressions were read at the party. When I asked her about her memories of them, she said the first two that stuck out in her mind were from her brother Spencer who was away at college and from Mr. Ferrin, the person who fixed everything at our house over the years. We loved it when he visited.

Erika recalled Mr. Ferrin had written in his letter that she was a special person with a good heart. He wrote that when he would come to our house to work, she always greeted him and visited with him. He went on to say that at many of the other houses he worked in, most of the children would walk by him like they didn't see him. From this comment, she learned how important a smile, a greeting, and a short conversation can mean to others. A point of interest in someone giving from the heart: Mr. Ferrin had been retired when he decided to go to work as a handyman. He saved the money he earned being an excellent handyman to put his grandchildren through college. Which, by the way, he has done. One grandchild is planning on going on to become an attorney and the other is just finishing a nursing degree. He is a rather quiet and gentle person, plus a hard worker.

The only man at the party was my friend's husband. They didn't realize the party was just for women. When it came time for him to say something to Erika, he delivered such a warm-hearted message that it left everyone in tears, including him. What an added bonus. And despite wanting to run out of the room when she first realized what was happening, Erika does look back at this gathering as the gift it was intended to be.

Looking at this example with Erika, you may feel inspired to enjoy more of your own types of celebrations and surprises of warmth and creativity for your children or others in your life. They are just thoughts away. A celebration can be as simple as a waking up in the morning and you telling your child or grandchild that this is their special day and let inspiration carry you into creative adventures.

Bucket Lists

Another fun tradition is to help children compile a "bucket list," and have them update it from time to time. Younger children will need your help. Yes, I know, we think of a bucket list as something adults compile as their wish list of desired future adventures and experiences. Just the same, I think we can invite children to start anticipating adventures they would like to experience. Why not? Even a three-year-old can begin to understand making a list with a bit of your encouragement. Be open to varied types of additions to the list from small interests to larger interests. Let them put anything on the list! Here is where creativity and imagination can walk in to help with this project. You could start this concept by gathering the family and doing a family bucket list, first. Again, remember to not give reasons why some of the ideas will or won't work. Maybe they want to fly to the moon. Simply have them put it down. Maybe they are 10 years old at the time, but the dream stays as a constant on their lists over the years. This may be their top goal, which leads them into different interests and studies. Maybe they ultimately become an astronaut. In other words, the sky is the limit for additions on these lists from their heart and imaginations. It's not your job to limit the options for the bucket list.

From these projects, children will learn how to plan for achieving their wishes: the value of money and saving it, investigating and working towards something that is important to them, and learning their goals may change over time. There are so many ways children can benefit from a bucket list. For a small child, perhaps they want a toy. When the kids were growing up and they wanted something, I would tell them to put it on their wish list. If they saved their money, they could get it early. Or it might be their favorite birthday present or Christmas present that year. If they had ten items on this list, then it gave them a chance to pick their top one or two. In this step, prioritizing and practicing decision-making is employed. Constant immediate gratification is not the main theme here—although some sprinkles of it can be healthy and fun.

VIRTUAL MEETINGS AND CONNECTING ACROSS THE MILES

Where do We Fly Tonight?

One of the things I started doing with Jessie Bean, who is now 10, is meeting each other on many nights to go places. Let me tell you what I mean. This all started when she was about five years old, and she was so sad when I would leave to return home or she would leave after a visit. We started a tradition when we visit with each other on the phone. We will plan to fly and meet each other for adventures each night. First we plan where we would like to go, such as a beach or a picnic in a forest. We think about what we want in our picnic basket. Oftentimes her older sister would participate if she was close by.

To give you an idea of how these adventures start, one of us will ask, "What are you flying on tonight?" Jessie Bean might answer, "I'm flying on a pig that has tons of sparkles on it, and its nails are all painted different colors with jewels on them. Its tail is a rainbow." My turn, and I might say, "I'm flying on a flamingo that is purple with orange dots, with a large diamond around its neck that is catching all the colors that are radiating up to us. The diamond sends them back out into the night sky to play with the shimmering stars to light our way." This night when we asked her sister Madi if she would like to come, she yawned and said, "I'm going to fly on the biggest bed ever! I'm exhausted from school." We all laughed with the idea of landing in Maui. We were tickled to think how the bed was going to be received as it landed on the sandy beach with all of us, plus the radiant pig and the sassy flamingo! We figured by the time we arrived it would be the middle of the day. The bed really was comically out of place!

In the last year or so, we have advanced to picking exact places like Australia, Chile, and different states in the US like California. Then we would pick a real city or beach within these larger locations. Jessie started finding them on the map in her room. Sometimes her mom and sister would help her look up these places, but she has quickly become proficient on her own. We now have broadened to Google Maps. We jointly look up the same locations on our computers and travel to cities and backroads together investigating the different cultures, peoples, living conditions, and terrains, while looking up data about these locations and countries while on FaceTime. This ritual has us feeling like we get to see each other while traveling the world.

And, yes, we do continue our beloved tradition of flying on something unique to get to these places. I don't think we will ever give up on our flights of fancy.

Learning and Sharing Across the Miles

Long distance, Madi and I have looked up different subjects up online, and we share the information with each other which leads to great discussions. There is no lack of knowledge and ideas at our fingertips. It is a refreshing way to connect with grandchildren and to expand learning at the same time. We aren't in the same town, and this gives us another way of building a tradition between the two of us.

Interactive Games Across the Miles

When I answered my cell phone, it showed my daughter was FaceTiming me. To my surprise, it was Greyson (six years old) with a big grin on his face. He stated, "Grandma, I called you all by myself. All I have to do is push M-O-M on my mom's iPad, and I get you." I said, "What does M-O-M spell?" He stated, "I don't know. I just have to remember to push the M-O-M." This call, and a number of calls since, have us spending curiously clever time together.

The first time Greyson called me like this, I had three little elves on the table. We have ended up enjoying many a game with them hiding around the house, with Greyson trying to find them as I walk around showing him the many hiding places. At one point, he said, "This is more fun than a video game, isn't it, Grandma?" If you try this, you can find many things to hide like rocks, stickers, marbles, pennies, etc. Greyson would say, "Grandma, close your eyes and count to 20 to see if they hide, again."

Just a couple of weeks ago when I was going to visit Greyson, now age seven, he firmly requested, "Grandma, why don't you stick two of those tricky elves in your pocket and bring them here. If we are really quiet and watch for them, maybe we can catch them running around on their cute little legs."

Artwork through the Ether

One day when Greyson called to FaceTime, Grandpa Jim was home, and Greyson wanted Grandpa Jim to draw for him. I held the cell phone while Greyson expertly encouraged Grandpa to draw his imagined creative concept ideas for a cat barn and surrounding yards. This took about 20 minutes. Grandpa Jim now limits the FaceTime drawing time to one-and-a-half hours a session on the phone. When they are together, they draw for several hours per session.

Secrets

On other FaceTime calls, Greyson has been telling me about different secrets and adventures in his life. It's a grand way to connect over the miles while building a relationship and memories.

Reading to Each Other

Another idea is a grandparent can read a bedtime story, tell them a story, sing a song to them, or say a prayer with them at bedtime using your video chat of choice. Jessie Bean, 10 years old, is reading chapter books to me over the miles.

The daughter of a friend of mine had twins five months ago, and my friend and her husband have committed to doing bedtime stories and other activities with this family's four-year-old (the twins' older sibling) online. This is a beautiful way to stay connected across the miles while helping the parents of this busy household, plus giving the four-year-old much needed special attention.

Playing Music

Both girls, Jessie Bean and Madi, play the fiddle. I love to have them entertain me on FaceTime. It is a great way for their practice time to be completed and for me to enjoy time with them.

What new traditions can you come up with? Ask the children in your life what they might consider traditions with you. Again, it's recognizing and jointly plucking diamonds out of heartfelt moments and adventures in time. This awareness and verbalization of their importance in your lives brings a special meaning to these activities. It's a bond in sharing and creating! And, as you can see, it can be the simplest of moments that can count.

PART 4

THE PURPOSE AND BENEFITS OF
IMAGINATION AND CONNECTION

CHAPTER 13

HELPING CHILDREN FEEL FEELINGS, COPE, AND PROBLEM SOLVE

This book is about being captivated by the richness in imagination, creativity, and the desire for positive connections and outcomes with children and adults alike. This philosophy can stand on its own. But some of us need to see there are specific benefits for investing in many of the playful ways to spend time with their children. And there are ways that we can have lots of fun with children while having an overarching goal of helping them along in their development as human beings.

When talking about this book, one friend said, "I can see how many of these ideas could positively change a child's life. Envision a child sitting in their bedroom, the lights low, and no one really seeing the hopeful, yet sad desire of him wanting someone to see him, and spend time with him while loving him, and feeling he is special and worthwhile. Because of the lack of these types of exchanges, he has learned that the feeling of despair generally overrides his hopes. But he still has a glimmer of hope that he and his needs will be noticed, at least for a few moments."

I know many children and adults feel like this from time to time. Some may feel like this all the time. But the joy of positive and loving relationships, plus quality time spent with another, can go a long way in answering this type of yearning.

In these next chapters, I share insights that might be helpful in dealing with children and their unique personalities.

When Feelings of Boredom Come Knocking

It's important to note that feelings of boredom are not to be confused with the above example of lack of quality attention.

When children feel truly bored, despite having the attention they need, it is a good time to encourage them to come up with new ideas, interests, or remember past intrigues. When my grandchildren tell their parents they are bored, and start pushing a few buttons, the parents will say, "If you are that bored, I will come up with something for you to do: dishes, cleaning, scooping up dog poo, etc." It's amazing to see how fast their little minds start creating.

Another idea here is for children to start a list of ideas for "When I'm Bored." This can become a well-loved list. I would encourage you to let them be the ones who refer to the list at these times. I'm smiling because I just tried to put myself in a child's place in their moments of boredom and frustration. If someone said to me, even now as an adult, "Go and get your list and figure it out," in the moment, it would probably make me feel like I would never want to look at the list again even if I loved the list. But if I heard, "You have great ideas, I bet you will come up with something you want to do," maybe with an added hug or pat, the feeling for me would be much different. What about for you?

Jessie Bean, age 10-and-a-half, informed me, "Mom now has a list of ideas on the refrigerator for us to do if we say we are bored. I never say I'm bored now because the list is of things that she doesn't want to do! Like cleaning the toilets. So I'm always able to keep myself busy."

SELF-SOOTHING TECHNIQUES

In times of frustration, anger, irritation, or boredom, it is good for children to work through their feelings, and come up with many of their own solutions, depending on their age. They are learning how to "do" life, the practice of life. If you are the one coming up with most of the ideas to relieve their uncomfortable emotions, they miss a chance to practice and get used to the concept of self-soothing. For the purposes in this book, I'm using the term of "self-soothing" to encompass a broad range of strategies where children—as well as adults—utilize ways of dealing with or coping in different situations.

If children at a young age learn to be self-soothing with positive, interesting, and supportive preferences, this capacity will strengthen as they mature. If they have learned to work through situations rather than be rescued, at least part of the time, it helps them build self-confidence, inner strength, and diversity in problem solving.

What works for self-soothing techniques? Now, this is where, in my mind, things can get tricky with all of the various positive and negative choices. What if you are trying to allow a baby time to learn about self-soothing? You let them cry some, and maybe they start reaching for a little toy, the silky edge of a blanket, a special stuffed animal, or they are entertained by their own movements or their own voice sounds, which is ideal. Or maybe a parent will innocently try to help with this process, and they give the baby a bottle of milk or juice, or sit them in front of the television to work on the process. It doesn't take long before a baby knows if it keeps crying (after recently being fed, their diaper changed, and the parents know it isn't uncomfortable or frightened), they will be rewarded with a bottle or some type of electronics. On the surface, this looks like they are learning how to entertain themselves, but are they? Perhaps what they have really learned is something external is required to calm them down.

As children grow, how many times is food used to calm a child down when they are upset, hurt, or moody? When a child is bored, do they decide to fill this void by going to the kitchen and finding things to eat when they aren't really hungry? Does this become a pattern? Children learn some of their patterns from watching adults and seeing how they deal with emotions in different situations.

Many people consciously and unconsciously equate food with love, generosity, and support. Foods (especially desserts) can seem to magically help someone to feel better in the moment. How many times, in a movie, have you seen someone, oftentimes a woman, rush to the fridge for a container of ice cream or a bottle of wine to soothe her feelings after being jilted?

Stop here for a moment and think. What are your first, go-to activities, interests, or connections when you encounter a difficult or frustrating situation? Maybe riding your bike, reading a book, watching a movie, calling a friend, seeking spiritual support, going to work, playing an instrument, going for a drive, meditating, knitting, taking a nice hot bath, cleaning your house, working in the garden, building something, cooking, or eating may be some of your supportive choices. Which strategies do you feel will be advantageous for your children to incorporate in their lives as they mature?

The more we as adults are conscious of how we behave during our times of stress, the more we can help guide the children in our lives to choose life-giving strategies during difficult times.

So I hope it is evident to you at this point that all the suggestions in this book—time spent in creating interests, increasing connections with children, and learning to be fully engaged in one's life—helps children navigate life, especially the difficult and uncomfortable parts of life, and in the best possible ways. It does this by giving them a body of experiences, both internally and externally, that lead to agile abilities in dealing with life's stresses, frustrations, disappointments, challenges, and successes as they grow and mature. If a child learns to envision a whole world out of a nook in a tree or a leaf floating on a stream, they can more easily figure out how to reimagine stressful or frustrating situations and then ultimately be more able to move more comfortably in their growing worlds of changes and challenges.

So the question to ask ourselves is, do our coping abilities bring us closer to joy, peacefulness, and balance? Or do they end up adding to our frustrations?

JOY SKILLS

Coping skills or self-soothing skills are such clunky terms. So, let's playfully rename them. How does "Joy Skills" sound? Sounds good to me!

Identifying Feelings

Part of developing these joy skills is being able to name both comfortable and uncomfortable feelings. Identifying one's feelings is an essential skill in making life-affirming choices. Helping children expand their abilities to express and name their emotions can be lots of fun. Let me show you.

"Mom! I'm so exasperated!" four-year-old Isabelle strongly states as she throws her little hands out for an added effect. You see, her friend David borrowed her bike and hadn't returned it. I know, "exasperated" is a big word for a little one like Isabelle. As I mentioned in the Adventures chapter, many small children love to learn words and meanings. Parents oftentimes think they are too little to understand, let alone use them. I'm challenging you to experiment with the idea of trying these next ideas. I believe you will be pleasantly surprised.

Helping Children to Expand Their Feeling Word Vocabulary

Help children expand their vocabulary of feeling words as they mature. Learning to understand these feeling words can become a family game. This could happen at the dinner table or during family time where one word is picked and everyone tries to explain it by facial expressions, body language, other words, and sounds. For an added bit of creativity in exploring words, my editor, Elaine, expressed her delight in how she loves the way some words feel in her mouth when she says them.

Think about the humor and lively discussions that might arise around these types of explorations. During the week, everyone can try using the chosen word at various times. Their ability to express themselves verbally as well as with body language will easily develop without a lot of effort. I challenge you to try this for a few weeks. I bet the whole family will look forward to these exchanges.

In Chapter 13, you will find a starter list of words that express feelings. Add more to the list by remembering favorite family ones or made-up ones. A made-up one we recognized at our house when the kids were growing up was "fitzer." To us, it meant being highly frustrated while having a bit of a fit. I must admit, it wasn't always my children's favorite one if it popped up in the midst of them expressing a bit of exasperation. In one of my friend's family, they came up with the word, "ruper." It means amazing, wonderful, way beyond super-duper. If someone uses that word to describe a feeling or situation, everyone knows they are talking about something very, very good! Kids will have fun making up words to fit some of their feelings. Watch out, they may become your family's favorites.

Exploring Feelings with a Charades Card Game

Make cards with feeling words and supporting facial expressions on one side of the card. This can become a family project. Children will have fun helping with the cards, and this deck can be added to as the young ones mature. This game can be especially helpful with anger, hurt, fear, and other painful feelings. Children oftentimes feel it is wrong to have these feelings. What a sense of freedom to learn to be able express their whole range of feelings while gradually learning to express them in acceptable ways! Plus, they are learning to recognize others' variations in ways of expressing feelings. What a monumental gift to all involved.

I would start out with a few simple words and cards for feelings in the beginning. You will know when to add new ones. The cards you create for this game will probably be treasured by the family, especially the cards the children made when they were little.

The ultimate benefit of these next two games is the children start recognizing their feelings more clearly. Then they start to express them in clearer ways rather than pouting, screaming, hitting, or disengaging.

CHARADES, GAME 1: The first person picks a card, and they try to come up with a facial expression to match the feeling on the card. Little kids may need some help in the beginning, but they will learn fast. At this point, everyone at the table can try to guess the emotion. It can lead to a number of different discussions about feelings and how to express them. When was the last time someone felt the feeling or they saw someone else act out the feeling? What does it feel like to have the feeling? I can easily see this happening at mealtimes. It will add humor and connection with those at the table. This game can easily end up as a loved tradition.

CHARADES, GAME 2: Make an acting game out of how to handle different emotions between two people. The difference in this second game of Charades is everyone in the game knows what emotion is on the card. The cards can also have situations on them like "Molly took my bike," "Jason hit me," or "Emma ate my sandwich." The person who picks the card will act out the feeling, and the second person will respond.

In thinking through this game, the two parties can first act out the positive role play or negative role play for varied ways of dealing with an emotion.

In this example below, a parent figure tells a child figure that they have to stop playing because they have to leave to go to the store. Feelings that may come up are: anger, frustration, and hurt. NOTE: A lot of times, anger comes after an initial feeling, like feeling hurt or left out.

Negative Expressions

The first party may cross their arms tightly around themselves, and then say something like: "I don't like you." "I never want to see you again." "I hate you!" "Leave me alone." "I want to hit you." They may follow this up with sticking their tongue out or pretending to throw something.

Second party might say, "I don't like you either." Or: "You leave me alone." They may stamp a foot to make their point.

Positive Expressions

First party may still cross their arms or stick their hands in their pockets. They might say, "I don't like being told I have to stop playing." "I feel angry when you abruptly tell me to stop something, when I feel I need or want to do something else."

The second party doesn't react to the anger, but instead

acknowledges it and explores the reason for it. They may also offer a solution: "You look angry." "What I hear you saying is you are very upset that I asked you to stop playing." "Let's talk about it." "I may understand you better if you explain." "What would make this work better for you in the future when I need you to do something else?"

First party, "What about warning me ahead of time that I will need to do something else like in 10 minutes?"

Second party: "That sounds like a perfect idea."

(If you are interested in learning more about active listening skills, take a look at any good parenting book or website.)

The audience can give them support, guidance, or help in coming up with ideas on how to express and deal with the different emotions after the two participants are finished demonstrating their parts. This can be quite informative and funny for children to watch two adults when they are the two participants acting out the emotion and how to deal with it. Adults' hearts will be touched by the sincerity and playfulness of children in these games.

A word of caution, if your child starts using the negative ways of dealing with their feelings, and you surmise they learned them in the role-playing exchanges, you may have to give up that part of the game. To me, this is the part of the game they will find to be the funniest which keeps them enjoying the game while learning. But with this game, you can set it up anyway that works for your family. These suggestions are a starting place. You and your family's insights and imaginations, as well as your family's particular needs, will help you create your own versions. Young children will enjoy these games with encouragement and humor from adults in their lives. The games can grow with the age of the child.

Here are some words to describe feelings you might like to use when playing the Charades game or helping children learn new words of expressions:

HAPPY/GLAD/GOOD-FEELING WORDS:

amazed	brave	bubbly
calm	cheerful	comfortable
content	delighted	elated
enthusiastic	excited	fired-up
giddy	glad	grateful
joyful	kind	loved
mellow	nutty	optimistic
peaceful	pleasant	reassured
"ruper"	satisfied	strong
terrific	thankful	thrilled
valued		

SAD/HURT/PAINFUL-FEELING WORDS:

ashamed	awful	bad
blah	crushed	down
gloomy	hurt	lonely
miserable	powerless	rejected
rotten	sad	sorry
sorry	stupid	sulky
unhappy	unloved	upset

MAD/ANGRY/UPSET-FEELING WORDS:

ashamed	awful	bad
blah	crushed	down
"fitzer"	gloomy	hurt
lonely	miserable	powerless
rejected	rotten	sad
sorry	stupid	sulky
unhappy	unloved	upset

FEAR FEELING WORDS:

alarmed	fearful	nervous
petrified	scared	terrified
trembly	uneasy	unsure
worried		

OTHER FEELING WORDS:

bold	bored	capable
confident	creative	curious
disorganized	embarrassed	energetic
fired-up	foggy	friendly
guilty	hesitant	jealous
lazy	mixed-up	optimistic
perplexed	preoccupied	proud
sassy	shaky	shy
skeptical	small	strong
super	tired	understood
unsure	weak	weird

CHAPTER 14

THE CHALLENGE OF RAISING CHILDREN IN THE AGE OF EVER-PRESENT ELECTRONICS

This chapter can be easily summarized by simply saying that there is significant scientific evidence that children's overuse of electronics is a detriment to them and their developing brains.

If you would like to refresh or broaden your knowledge in support of this idea or need ideas on how to limit screen time, please read on. If you are familiar with the hazards of children spending too much time in front of screens, joyfully skip to the next chapter.

There is no getting around the fact that we are challenged by the balance between use and misuse of the relatively new and ever-increasing lure of electronics. It is of value to illuminate both the pros and the cons of usage and its effects in our children's worlds, our world, and the worlds with others we engage.

Advantages

We all know the advantages are vast for the uses of electronics like computers and cell phones. Their value in work environments is extremely supportive in time management, knowledge, connections, and supporting an edge of competitiveness to mention a few. Outside the work environment, a world of information is at our fingertips which can increase knowledge, curiosity, and new interests: calendars, exercise and relaxation sites, music and news are assets if managed. Virtual connections across the miles have become one of my favorite uses of technology, as you have come across earlier in this book with exchanges with children in my life.

I was first introduced to Skype when my son Spencer was stationed in Mosul during the Iraq War. He was set up to Skype with Madi, his then-two-year-old daughter, while being away from her. During his absence, she came to visit at my mom and dad's house, and Spencer called on the phone from Iraq. When she started to talk to him without Skype, she was being demonstrative in her actions like waving her hands around, taking different poses and making faces. I looked at her mom questioningly, and Jenny explained, "She is used to talking to him on Skype where he can see her."

Disadvantages

The most alarming disadvantage, from my point of view is that these shiny electronic devices have insidiously replaced more and more of our interactive human connection time, including with children, family, friends and acquaintances.

The weekend I was contemplating writing this chapter, my husband and I were driving through parts of Montana. We saw lots of evidence of the noxious weed, leafy spurge which has been spreading its beautiful, tiny, but abundant yellow blossoms for miles and miles. It looks so innocent and pleasantly alluring. It is a gift to the honeybees! On the flip side, it grows densely, and chokes out almost anything in its destructive, seemingly unrelenting path. This destroys the diversity of the landscape where wildflowers, grasses, and many bushes once flourished. They are now being replaced by this devastating and unrelenting weed.

This weed reminds me a bit about the worrisome possible effects of overuse of electronics for both children and adults including: numbing feelings; taking time away from one to one interactions with others; decreasing imagination; decreasing diversity in interests and passions; increasing psychological issues; and increasing physiological issues such as obesity and orthopedic problems, to mention a few. It can decrease the spontaneity and richness of our children's responses as they mature. There is a good chance they won't be spending as much time exploring or trying on as many new hats of life.

How does this over usage affect children's understanding of the fine nuances of their worlds? Will it affect their ability to interpret voice tones, body language, and facial expressions? I like to think these are evolving and maturing forms of recognition in engagements with others. In understanding one-to-one encounters, I think of it as a dance of personalities, wits, charm, and characters unfolding. Will children compare themselves and their lives to the standards of dress, home life, friends, and personalities they relate to on television and on the internet? Will some or much of this affect their self-esteem? Can that lead to mental health issues like depression? To me, with all the variables that go into fully interacting in person, and with the decreasing time spent learning the art of interpreting these exchanges, I wonder if this could create significant barriers. Do the young who have had less time spent interacting with electronics have an advantage over those who freely utilize electronics as their main way of spending free time?

Studies show using electronics creates changes in the brains of people of all ages; this is especially true in children. I would encourage you to explore the latest research and studies. I think most of us are aware of the effects of the overuse of these devices—including television—which can be detrimental and addictive.

When I was thinking through the idea of addictive patterns that can develop from the over-usage of electronics, I became concerned that children's nervous systems would become habituated to numbness rather than having them learning to deal more directly in interactions with others and life itself. How will this affect the quality and finesse of children's interactions and choices as they mature?

Modeling Behavior

Let's look at the quality of the time spent by parents, babysitters, and other adults who are using cell phones, computers, and television while spending time with children or with other adults. Are they really spending time together or lulling themselves into thinking they are because they are in the same room or on the same outing? Our worlds seem busier than ever. Two (or more) incomes are often needed for a family to survive. There are many single parent families. Parents can be tired at the end of the day, and they welcome having their children occupied in this world of electronics while they get dinner on, finish chores, and try to relax for a few moments. There can be a nice feeling of things settling into a relatively calm routine in many households with everyone in their own worlds.

I became a single parent when my children were five and twelve years old. I worked full time, plus I went back to school for my master's degree. I must say it was a balancing act and not always easy. I look back with smiles and love, and I hope I spent enough time with each of them. I know we had video games, but I don't remember them being overused.

It is important to acknowledge that the overuse of electronics can result in decreased connection. Ask yourself, what is excess? Where is the balance? If you look at the example above, how might a routine evening like this one be altered to support everyone involved?

Ideally, everyone could help get things ready for evening dinners, and help with chores. Family time during the meals might include visiting, maybe word games, current events shared, and always a sincere "How was your day?" No cell phones, if possible. Game nights once or more a week? Add in some one-on-one moments, and the formula is pretty complete. Time left over can be used for everyone enjoying their own personal choices of electronics, homework, getting together with friends, or a hobby.

In thinking about this chapter, I thought a lot about the children I worked with professionally over the years especially the ones I worked with for five years in Rivendell, which was the most restrictive in-patient psychiatric center for youth in Montana, at the time. I co-counseled a survivors' group with a psychologist for about two years, and then I ran a survivors' group for the next three years. I loved my time working with these young people. I could easily see past their hurts and losses and see their beautiful spirits, and understand their hopes of being protected, understood, cared for, and heard.

To watch many of their transformations over the weeks and months they spent at the facility was remarkable. I think one of the key components was the quality and caring of the time individually spent with them by professionals and peers.

Several years ago, I had a young man come up to me and say, "I wanted to thank you and tell you how my life changed with the support and encouragement from you and my therapist during the time I spent at Rivendell. I graduated from high school, I am married and have two children, and I have a good job. I am the first person who isn't an alcoholic in generations in my family."

This is an example of how spending interactive, connected time with children and others can bring joy and solidness which can help them flourish.

Engaging Children and Setting Boundaries on Electronics

The real question is how to engage children when they are involved in the mesmerizing usage of electronics where the child is isolated and detached.

Is the solution easy? One would think the simple answer would be to offer different activities, games, or adventures. But, at this point, what you might hear, more often than not, is:

"I don't have time right now." "Maybe later!" "Mom, I'm busy." "That doesn't really interest me." "I can't concentrate on my video game when you keep asking me questions." "That may sound interesting to you, but it isn't to me."

After really thinking though this dilemma, I believe setting boundaries on daily time with the isolating effects of electronics, spending quality time with children, and having them come up with different interests and activities they are drawn to are some of the solutions that will bring the most success over time.

How do you do that when it seems, like for many, the electronics feel like a lifeline, their best friend?

You start first by having a talk with each child. Let them know why you are limiting the usage, and what they will gain. Even three-and four-year-olds will understand this discussion, at some level. It's important they understand it's not a punishment, but a gift.

I know you have a lot of ideas on the benefits of setting limits. These are a few possibilities which came to mind for me:

🦋 You will have more quality time together.

🦋 They will end up with more interests.

🦋 They will have more time to engage in person with friends.

🦋 They will thrive on the benefits of their creative interests.

🦋 They'll have more fun exploring new skills, and choosing ways of interacting in and with life.

🦋 They will become more inclined to be doers rather than watchers.

🦋 They will become more internally motivated rather than externally motivated.

🦋 All in all, spending less time with electronics will lead to increased joy and engagement!

If children are resisting, you will initially need to remind them that you have their best interests at heart. They probably won't believe you at first; you have taken away one of their favorite activities. You may end up dealing with a moody, angry, unhappy child who will try to push your buttons. This is normal. It makes the best of us want to give in and not follow through with boundaries we have set. The best gift you can give them, and yourself, is to keep a firm boundary!

Most of us don't like someone else changing something we are completely happy with and don't have any desire to change. Please be patient with them. Within reason, let the child decide when and how they would like to use the allotted electronic time doing things like video games and television. This will empower them, and they will be learning more about choices, savoring, and enjoying the feeling they have a say in how their time unfolds.

The moments of our lives seem infinite, but ultimately are limited in richness collectively depending on choices. Help your child see that each moment with eyes glued to the world on a screen is a moment lost in the world around them. Oh, and lovingly remind yourself of that too!

CHAPTER 15

TRIED AND TRUE PARENTING ADVICE: CHOICES AND CONSEQUENCES

When I was a new mom, I received several pieces of very good advice which really helped me raise my children. They were:

Pick the top three parenting books that are available and read each one of them for understanding the different stages of development and for child-rearing approaches.

Watch friends and family whose parenting you have admired. Take a parenting class.

Find a doctor you trust to look to for advice.

After years of raising children and being a grandmother, I have since learned so much since my early days of parenthood. Here are a few parenting concepts I found helpful while I was raising my children. They have steadfastly withstood the test of time. I have considered them gifts that helped make parenting much easier while respecting the child's independent and unique maturing spirit.

1. Let Their Own Internal Approval Reign

When my son was five years old, I read a tip on parenting that made such clear sense to me, it had me sitting down with my son the very next day. I was hoping I hadn't already ruined him by turning him into a people pleaser, meaning he would go through life needing other people's approval to really feel good about himself. The article said when children constantly hear praise from their parents and other people around them, they continue to need this praise as they grow into adulthood to feel good about themselves. Instead, it encouraged parents and other adults to frequently ask children about how "they feel" about what they have accomplished rather than impose a judgement upon them. This is the idea of being internally motivated rather than externally motivated. So, the next day when I sat him down, the conversation went a little bit like the following. I straight forwardly said, "Honey, your Dad and I are going to change the way we have been doing something with you. You know how we are always telling you how well you do in a lot of things and how wonderful you are?" He nodded a yes. So, I continued on, "In the future, we will only be saying things like that part of the time." He just stared at me. "Going forward, we will be asking you, part of the time, how you feel about different things you have done or accomplished. This will help you to grow up to rely on yourself and what you think, rather than needing other people's approval. Just know your dad and I will always be feeling you are doing great. Do you have any questions?" "No, it's fine mom, I get it," he quietly answered. I think he understood this conversation and took it to heart as much as any five-year-old could. Did I say he grew up to be an independent person, with a strong grounded personality and an immensely kind and giving heart?

2. Choices and Natural Consequences

I think it's crucial for children to learn to be responsible for their choices and realize their actions will bring natural positive or negative consequences. Even though children realize there will be consequences for their negative actions, it doesn't mean they will be happy about the outcomes. When I emphasized this bit of insight and wisdom with my children, I generally heard, "Mom, I hate it when you say choices and consequences!" or "Mom, don't say consequences one more time! It makes me mad when you say I made the choice!" I inwardly smiled and continued on with the natural consequence of the moment. In their defense, as you already surmised, I generally shared this wisdom at the times when they ended up with a consequence they weren't happy about.

A "natural" consequence is a consequence or outcome that is as close to the choice they made or are thinking of making. One good example: The son of one my friends used some crayons on the lower wall for his art board. We were sitting at the kitchen table when my friend discovered this. She calmly asked which one of her children had designed this impressive graffiti. When the culprit was discovered, she simply handed him some paper towels and cleaning spray and said, "We don't color on the walls. You will need to clean it up." We continued visiting as we watched him out of the corner of our eyes struggling to remove his heartfelt strokes of design. Did I mention he was two years old? I was amazed he actually attempted to do it, and he stuck with it without complaining or trying to get out of it. I guess he knew the rules at that young age. And I bet he never tried it again. One of the important parts of this way of handling choices and consequences is to be calm and not be critical or angry.

Giving them a time-out to think about what a better choice would be the next time is fine if there isn't something that seems like a natural consequence to enact first, like cleaning up the drawing on the wall. I often used time out and consequences together. This can be from sitting on the floor, in a chair, or going to their room depending on their age and your child. For older children, you might ask them to write about a better choice for the next time; or have them write an affirmation, and they can write it over a certain number of times. At the end of this time, you can have a small visit with them about what they thought about. Some brainstorming with them about how to handle situations differently may be in order depending on their choice, their understanding, and their need for your input or not.

Starting or following a consequence with labeling certain negative comments (like "You have been a bad boy or girl!" "That was really bad!" "Shame on you." "What's wrong with you?") is a way of trying to get messages across to children, but these types of comments that label the situation or the child as bad or shameful can erode their self-esteem. Children are so literal. They can end up thinking they are bad boys and girls all the time. They might think they should be ashamed in general. Even the idea of having a special chair labeled "Bad boy chair" or "Bad girl chair," I feel, delivers a negative message to them.

Another key part of this approach is using the word "consequence" rather than "punishment." "Punishment" brings with it the idea you are bad rather than you are learning about changing an action. I know, they are just two words, but stop a moment and try them out on yourself. Which one brings the idea of learning while leaving your self-esteem intact? Which one makes you feel like you are a little less and not okay?

And lastly, an important part of this learning process for children is for adults to be consistent in setting boundaries followed by fair consequences. This way the child knows what to expect and learns to make choices that lead to desired positive consequences or outcomes. These ways of thinking and feeling through their choices and coming up with decisions that support their situations in any given moment matures with the child as they grow into adulthood.

I thought this a great example of a child learning to make choices:

> Greyson, six years old at the writing of the book, was visiting at my house. It was time to put on sunscreen, and he wasn't happy about me trying to put it on him. I asked if he would like to put it on himself or have me do it. He wanted to learn to do it himself. (This is an example of an empowering choice.) The first time he tried to put on the sunscreen, I guided him a lot. If he missed spots, I helped—which he didn't appreciate. I let him know that once he learned how to completely cover his face, then I wouldn't need to help. The second time, he was getting better, and I only helped a little. He worked very hard on learning this skill. The third time, he looked at me and stated, "This is getting a lot easier. I like putting it on myself." He didn't need my help at all. I complimented him on his success.
>
> A day later, he looked at me with concern in his eyes, "Grandma, if my parents know that I know how to put my own sunscreen on, they will be telling me to do it!" I simply said, "Let's think through this. If they are asking you to put sunscreen on, would this mean you were going to be going outside?" He said, "Yes." I then asked, "Then this would mean that you would need to have sunscreen on before you go outside?" He said,

"Yes." I then asked, "Would you rather have them put your sunscreen on, or would you rather do it yourself? He emphatically stated, "I don't like it at all when other people put on my sunscreen. I want to do it myself!"

Through this process, the choice for a positive outcome presents itself. Does he like the thought of needing to use sunscreen? No, but he does know that it is the choice if he wants to go outside.

3. The Joy of Moving Through Life with Integrity

"Mom, look!" Erika excitedly thrust out a large hand of gem-like, multicolored round pieces of gum. "I put my penny in the machine, and I pulled the lever again and again, and I just kept getting pieces of gum. Her face was radiant. We were driving in the car, at this point. I gently stated, "Honey, you can keep these if that is what you decide, but it sounds like the gum machine was broken. The people at the store don't know what happened. Think about what feels best to you inside."

After a month of the gum sitting in a little cup on her windowsill, Erika came to me and said she wanted to go back to the store and leave enough money to pay for the gum. Even if they didn't know, she knew. I was so proud of her, at that moment! I'm not sure she ever ate any of that gum.

About four months later, when I picked her up at the racket club where she was taking her tennis lessons, she all but flew into the car with excitement, "Mom, guess what happened?! I put my quarter in to get a bag of chips, but when it came out there was another one with it. I went to the desk and handed the extra one to the lady and told her what happened. She said, "And you are giving it back? Not many children would do that. Thank you for being so honest. You just keep it and enjoy it." Erika smiled all the way home. We did talk about how good it feels when you are honest about something, even if no one would have known what happened.

4. The Freedom of Limited Choices

A lot of parents, maybe you included, are constantly in ongoing struggles with things like the kids not wanting to go to bed, not wanting to put on their coats, or refusing to brush their teeth. Well, this was another simple tip I learned along the way. If you ask a child a question like, "Do you want to put on your coat now?" or "Do you want to get up in your chair?" or "Will you pick up your toys?" or "Will you brush your teeth?" then they have the right to answer "Yes," "No," or "Not now." You asked them the question, and generally they say "No," and this can lead to them being upset when you say something like, "Do it now." And then, in turn, you may become a little upset or irritated as the bargaining begins.

The trick is to give them a different kind of choice rather than "Yes" or "No." Frame it like this: "Do you want to put on your coat now or do you want me to put it on?" They may still refuse but then they soon learn you will follow through and help them put it on, while saying, "You made this choice by not doing it yourself." They do get irritated when you tell them it was their choice, but it doesn't take them long to understand they do have the choice between outcomes. The best part, as the adult, is you feel a little more confident that in time things will get easier. Follow through with this kind of approach is the hardest when you are tired or preoccupied, but worth the effort in the long run.

5. Let Go of the Need for Neatness

The final piece is to try a dose of my mother's refreshing and loving wisdom: don't worry so much about the kids making a mess when exploring their environments and their creativity.

Bonus for Parents and Adults:
Choices and Decisions Throughout Life

My exploration of the meaning and wisdom of choices and how they impact us began when a friend of mine told me about her story of meeting her wonderful husband and their decision, after weighing their choices, to get married. They did this even though their circumstances were complicated at the time.

My friend has had a number of people tell her that they wish they had the same type of relationship in their lives. She always tells those people that it may seem that her relationship was and is obviously meant to be, but at the time that she and her husband met, it took a very specific choice on each of their parts to even contemplate entering into a relationship. So even though it was not convenient, expected, or imagined by either of them beforehand, they decided to trust the gift that was presented to them. My friend says that, in a way, they both felt that their only choice was to choose the love and deep connection that was present between them. And yet, at the same time, it was a bold and brave decision after weighing their other commitments in their lives.

Being a romantic, I love their story and their very apparent love, respect, support, and abundance of happiness that continues to be expressed between the two of them. But more importantly, I started pondering the difference between choices, decisions, and outcomes. Are they one and the same? How do we learn to make many of our choices and decisions that eventually lead to the directions our lives take? Are setting boundaries a part of this equation? Where do desires, wants, and needs fit into our decision-making processes—or do they at all? Where do learned "shoulds," limitations, and fears fit in? Is inaction or procrastination a choice?

Are there concrete answers to these questions? Does one answer fit for everyone?

I'm sure that it took you no time at all to think that the simple answer is these processes and outcomes are simply different for everyone.

Given this part of the book is about how we form opinions and evaluate our choices that lead to our decisions that ultimately usher in consequences, outcomes, and boundaries, I thought I would include the process I went through to try and discover for myself the best answer.

I found these thoughts brought me to the place of asking more questions, and playing with different outcomes and ideas. The journey expanded over a few days as I contemplated an ever-growing list of possibilities. If we were all sitting down together, I can only imagine the lively, diverse discussion that would unfold.

How do we learn to evaluate choices that ultimately lead to the decisions we make in our lives? Do we feel a strength and assurance in our ability to anticipate the consequences of our choices that lead to both positive and negative outcomes? How do we learn to gather information to empower us to learn how to wisely create the moments in our lives? How do we learn the skills in making choices and decisions? Are they learned or innate skills? Are we flexible in fine-tuning these skills over our lifetime or do we always fall back on the same set of patterns?

Do our decision-making skills lead to empowering us to create an ease in life that finds happiness and a richness of abundance in living? What do we bring in our toolbox of skills to create our choices? Do we feel a flexibility in our ability to navigate life? Do we "trust our gut" in making decisions, like the couple above?

Are we inspired to feel the freedom and innovation of stepping beyond our learned ways of thinking and viewing opportunities? Can we walk in lightness and mindfulness at the same time? Can intentions and choices support, affect, and embolden high self-esteem; increase happiness; bring balance and growth in outcomes; enhance ways of engaging with life and others; and support creativeness and curiosity in expanding our lives?

Is taking responsibility for one's decisions important? Is there validation and understanding for supporting oneself through learning curves? Will we always make perfect decisions?

In looking further, how do we find stability in our lives? How are we connected to others and our worlds? Do we have an ease in making decisions that seem to naturally flow? How do we become increasingly more comfortable with our choices?

Do we always realize we are analyzing choices that lead to our decisions? When needed, how do we fine-tune an ability to stop and think about our choices, decisions, and outcomes? How does being internally empowered rather than externally controlled when making decisions affect one's life? Do we understand our unconscious learned expectations and limitations? Do we actually stop and ask ourselves what truly feels right, at this time?

Is your youthful heart still very much alive and looking for creative options in choices and decisions? Are your choices liberating? Do they feel like breaths of fresh air as well as being in your best interest? Do they create joy, and are they rewarding? Are they your heart's desires? Where does being spontaneous fit in?

Are decisions big and life-changing, or are they small and in the moments we are living? Where is the balance between immediate gratification versus achieving long term goals? How do positive and negative self-soothing choices play in our decision-making processes?

How do we learn to make choices that lead to our decisions that take into consideration boundaries and consequences in both the long and short term that lead to our dance with life itself? When choices for adults or children are controlled through guilt, "shoulds," or fear, are they really choices? How does the need for decisions coming from these types of control affect one's self-esteem and thinking processes in making choices?

Having choices doesn't always mean that everything is flowing the way a person would like; however, to have the reasoning skills to make the best choices in any given situation is rewarding. We are all making many choices during a day: what to eat and not eat; do we exercise or not; do we accomplish what we set out to do; what is our attitude in thoughts and encounters? Do we have choices over our attitudes? Do these choices make a difference in outcomes?

How are our opinions formed that lead to the outcomes in decisions? Are attitudes just learned choices in ways of interacting with ourselves, others, and our worlds?

Just knowing and remembering we have choices, even over the smallest of things in our days is exhilarating and emancipating!

If we think about how we dance with the art form of choices and decisions, and how they influence outcomes that form our lives, we can smile and respect our intelligence and willingness to work with the puzzles that are handed to us in any given moment. And from there, we are in a good position to pass these varied skills on to the children in our lives.

CHAPTER 16

CHILDREN ARE TO BE SEEN AND HEARD

In dealing with children, treating them as equals is a monumental gift that will serve them well their whole lives as well as establish a rich and expanding relationship between you and the child as they grow. When they are treated with respect from an early age, and they know their opinions count and feel understood, children will blossom over time. Treating children with balance and respect goes a long way towards them thriving as adults. They will grow to expect and gravitate towards these same types of exchanges with others.

Granted, children do need the guidance and boundaries that are set by adults. That is understood. But the way the guidance and rules are dispensed can make all the difference in the child's responses and what they are feeling. The best insight or advice I can give you is to stop and think about how you would like incoming messages directed to you if you were the child you are guiding. Another way is to visualize how you would like—and allow—someone else to treat your child.

Oftentimes, parents are frustrated, tired, and pushed to their limits, and so they will yell or express their negative feelings with body language. They may verbally reach the "what's the matter with you" stage and shut the child down like the child is a dislikable monster that lives under the bed. In turn, the child rebels and acts out even more because they are hurt by the way the instructions and boundaries were delivered. I know, we are only human, but the more we can remember, in these challenging moments and in happy moments too, that these changeable, limit-resisting characters are the most precious of gifts in our lives, the more we can learn to use patience and love to deliver our consequences and boundaries more of the time.

This brief chapter is most importantly about exploring the idea of how we interact with the children in general. Examine your feelings about your role as the rule and boundary maker. Does it cause you anxiety because you feel a heavy responsibility trying to ensure they develop into responsible, happy adults? This can cause you to rule with a heavier hand than you would like. If the child views the parent or grandparent as a powerful authoritarian, they may fear the adult at some level. They may be leery of doing something wrong, or not living up to the adult's expectations, which, in turn, means to them that the adult will be disappointed and the adult's love could go away. Children are like puppy dogs, they want to get it right and please you, but their youthful eyes cannot yet see all options, and their underdeveloped "stop" buttons intertwined with their enthusiasm may get the better of them when making some of their decisions. It may be helpful to have knowledge of age-related developmental stages children pass through. This will give you increased insight and understanding in their changing worlds of growth.

There are many ways to interact with children, but one of the keys, I believe, is the respect in treating them with equality. This simply means you treat them with understanding, protection, wholesomeness, encouragement, humor, respect, and set healthy boundaries that are delivered with patience and love. There is an art in walking the seemingly thin tightrope of being a child's friend and playmate and equal, at times, and being the adult and parent, at other times.

Again, I feel the trick is simple—put yourself in the child's place. How would you like to be treated? How would you feel in different situations? What would you have liked done differently when you were a child? As an adult, how do you feel when you aren't treated as an equal, when your feelings are dismissed or not acknowledged, when someone cuts you off or tells you "not now"?

I'll share an example of a child trying to be heard. I called my son one morning when I was in Scotland on a trip and asked if he had any stories about Madi. She was six years old and in the first grade at a new school. He laughed, and said, "I actually have one from this morning. I was trying to get Madi ready for school, and I didn't want to be late for work. I was fixing her hair and asked her to get the barrette the fairies brought her. She said, 'I can't.' I said, 'Why?' and she said, 'I just can't.' We did this a couple of times, and I was getting a little frustrated, and said, 'Why not?' She looked up at me with determination is her eyes, and said, 'Because, I'm running with a real rough crowd down at that school, and you can't wear anything nice!'" After that exchange with her father, Madi felt she was heard, and she didn't wear the barrette to school.

My mother would say to me at times, "When we grew up, children were to be seen and not heard." I think in this day and age, children hold a much higher position in the ranks of healthy interactions. You already know many loving, intelligent ways of working with children that teaches them to respect themselves, as well as respecting others as equals. This support as they mature guides them to setting wise and healthy boundaries. Positive, solid self-esteem seems to come to them naturally. They are gradually guided by choices rather than the fear of doing something wrong or not getting it right. Maintaining a joyous, almost innocent love for life is one of their developing skills. This doesn't mean they aren't based in reality. Quite the contrary: they acknowledge and are educated about the fluctuating worlds around them. But they still resonate with feeling grounded, and they see and trust in their potential abilities to engage in the change flowing around them. A child treated with equality in interactions and spoken to with kindness and respect will find those same influences and qualities in their chosen relationships for rest of their lives.

This is a simple story I heard in a college class, and the wisdom of it has stuck with me over time. It is a lovely bit of common sense that I believe can resonate with many cultures and people.

Two Wolves

One evening, an old man told his grandson about a battle that goes on inside of all people. "My dear one, the battle between two 'wolves' is inside us all. One is evil. It is anger, fear, envy, jealousy, sorrow, regret, greed, arrogance, self-pity, guilt, resentment, inferiority, lies, false pride, superiority, and ego. The other is good. It is: joy, peace, love, hope, serenity, humility, kindness, benevolence, empathy, generosity, truth, compassion, and faith."

The grandson thought about it for a moment and then asked his grandfather, "Which wolf wins?"

The old man replied, "The one you feed."

PART 5

ADULTS NEED TO PLAY, TOO

CHAPTER 17

QUALITY TIME BEGINS WITH ONESELF (NOTES ON MINDFULNESS PART 1)

"Man is most nearly himself when he achieves the seriousness of a child at play." – HERACLITUS

Think about how children learn different ways of engaging in and with life. It is no different for us as adults if we want to add something new in our lives. The old saying, "What you put your time, attention, and energy towards is what will flourish," rings true in interacting with children or encouraging ourselves to bring something new into our lives. It is like beginning a new job, a new hobby, or a way of being in your world; it usually takes time and effort. Let's say you decided it would be fun to do some of the imaginary play captured in this book. Will you look at it and say, "Looks like a lot of worth-while fun, but I don't know how to do it, so I won't." Or, will you say, "I am going to generate that in my life with the kids. I'm intrigued by the heartfelt playfulness! I choose to rise to the occasion of the adventure of trying and creating something new." It will be like the challenging excitement of planning a summer vacation. Only you will be planning and learning some new interest or adventure. It will be worth the effort. Start out slowly, pick one or two ideas, and lightheartedly work with them until they are easily a part of your comfort zone.

THE ART AND PRACTICE OF BEING FULLY PRESENT

The way we give our loving attention to the children in our lives, in part, begins with us knowing how to give this to ourselves. The more adults (and even older teenagers) know how to create quality time in moments, the easier it will be for them to model and impart the essence of this gift more freely to the children in their lives. You may already know how to do this, or you may be questioning how to start effortlessly creating more of

these types of magical moments.

What if someone told you that you could be more fully engaged in your life with increased awareness and presence? What if it could start with a few minutes a day? What if those few minutes would easily increase your ability to feel the wonder of those around you and the richness of being? Would your heart smile with an interested curiosity?

What if I told you that you would, most likely, feel increased energy, expansive interests, a refined richness of liveliness, and increased satisfaction in exchanges with others and your world? Would that entice you to give it a try?

This way of interacting may become a refreshingly pleasant way of connecting at any time you choose. Don't be surprised if it becomes a desirable favorite habit. It's a bit like finding a fountain of energy and curiosity; the more you use these skills, the sooner they will become chosen, innate ways of exploring your connections with situations, activities, children, and other adults. I, personally, consider it an art form.

Hint: Start slowly with this gift to yourself. It is a slight shift in your perception in time. It is really that simple. Enjoy!

So, how does this work? What do you have to do?

Here is an example:

> As I sat down on the green glider on our porch on an early summer's day, I could hear the birds chirp warnings, encouraging me to honor their territory so they could protect their hatchlings. The sun's warm and soothing rays lightly danced over my face and body. The late morning dewdrops came alive with a brilliance of sparkles as they met the sun's welcoming greetings. I closed my eyes to gather more information: How did my feet and toes feel when they touched the deck to move me slowly back and forth? What did the gentle gliding feel like? The slight wind was gently touching my face and playfully blowing my hair which brought a small, slow smile to my lips. I opened my eyes and gazed and inspected the radiance of the varied flowers in the pots—colors, textures, and smells. I smiled and touched my face, then my hands. I rested my hands on my lap. The light pressure felt comforting and familiar. The texture of my jeans was slightly rough. I looked up and saw a few white clouds resting soothingly in the blue sky. My heart felt full and quietly happy in the richness and pure amazement of being fully present in these few short moments.

The nice surprise, after this small experiment on the porch, was the effects continued when I went into the house. My consciousness of the things around me took on a deeper illumination for a few extra minutes. I had simply slowed down long enough to be fully connected in mindfulness.

Hummingbirds at My Door?

You can also capture this kind of attention at odd moments in your day when you are jolted out of your routine and you are led to walk into increased awareness. This happened to me one early spring morning when the light was beginning to peek in around my curtains. I heard what I thought might be a little hummingbird at my bedroom door. It was the quietest of sounds, and then I heard it again.

I quietly opened my door as not to disturb anyone as it was four in the morning. To my surprise, there stood my friend Juliana who had spent the night! She sweetly smiled, and questioned as she walked into my room, "Are you awake? I just want to listen to the birds out your patio door. It is one of my favorite things to do in the spring." As we opened the door, we were greeted with an inspiring, beautiful orchestra of sounds that burst into the bedroom and into our hearts! She talked about the different bird sounds that she could identify as my heart filled with the joy of her childlike enthusiasm and playful happiness in knowing that she was sharing these moments with me. Before she left to go back to her bed, she perched almost like a small child on the side of my bed for a few minutes, and we pondered the mysteries and wonder of an early morning shared between two friends.

Since then, during the spring and early summer, I am now in the habit of opening my patio door to listen to the inspiring wild and delightful messages of life happening! My heart not only fills with the enchantment of the aliveness that greets me, but also the memories of spending those few minutes of full engagement with my cherished friend.

Your Turn: Experimenting with Engaging in the Moment

Find three to ten minutes. You can grab these minutes sitting in your car after you've reached a destination. They can be found after you finish your morning coffee or maybe after you've brushed your teeth at night. You'll be surprised to see how many tiny bits of time you can find once you are looking! Start using all of your five senses and your wide range of feelings to notice where you are at any chosen moment. Intently and peacefully investigate. This is almost like a wakeful meditation which means there isn't room for thinking about the next five activities you need to accomplish on your to-do list.

After playing with this aware state once or twice a day for about a week, I've come to the point where I just need to take a few slow breaths, tune into my five senses, and feelings, and I find I can be gently carried into a sense of refreshing presence at any time. It is a present to myself. I myself would like to become proficient at maintaining this state for longer periods of time. Initially I challenge you to try it out for just a few moments—you may become hooked by the freshness that awareness brings.

I don't suggest that this is a full-time objective, but a skill that will be increasingly and beautifully utilized when spending time with the children in your life and others around you. Being fully occupied in activities is important, but being fully enchanted in the radiance of children is the ultimate magic of connection for the purposes in this book.

So, let's do another experiment. Close your eyes for a minute or two and picture a scene where you are spending time with a child in your life. Do this before reading on.

Now, using the same scene, go back and really see the child and what you are doing together. Use your senses and feelings to complete this visualization for another couple of minutes. Really see the child you are with and feel your heart in capturing this scene. Please do this before reading on.

Next, I would like you to go back in this same scene and continue on from where you left off above. The new element to the scene is the phone rings, and you feel you need to answer it. The quick second you thought the phone call would take turns into several long minutes. You continue, almost absent-mindedly, interacting with the child while talking on the phone. Then you hear the washing machine beep as it beckons you to throw the laundry in the dryer. It will just take a second. On the way, you are thinking about the other things you need to do before dinner.

Take another couple of minutes completing this scene. And then read on.

Close your eyes one more time. Spend a little time and compare the two scenes. What is the child feeling in each situation? And what are you feeling?

These distractions and ways of connecting certainly happen between adults and children. And, as you already know, they also happen in adult-to-adult interactions. When we become aware of them and become aware of the effects they have on our relationships, we are able to make different, conscious choices.

Being in the Moment While Dating and Falling in Love

Dating and ultimately "falling in love" is one place where you may have had the opportunity to enjoy a deep level of sharing and connecting. This level of being connected in moments for extended periods of time is one of the most precious and memorable of gifts. Each party feels loved, seen, understood, and cherished. These seemingly magical connections, when broken down in a recipe, might include being thoughtful and wanting to know the other's feelings, needs, wants, and desires while equally feeling seen and heard by the other person. Add in the desire and follow-through by both parties for creating interesting times, adventures, and sharing of thoughts which adds to forming the container for the budding relationship. In this container, add in laughter, sprinkles of surprises, growing trust, and undivided special time together. These all add up to the increasing, heightened sense of wonder in everyday experiences. When you top all of this off with a touch of "chemistry" between two people, true magic unfolds.

Part of the beauty in these growing feelings is they are present regardless of what the couple is doing. They may simply be sitting on the porch, watching cars drive by while holding hands. On the surface this scene looks plainly nice and comfortable. But for the two people involved, the outward appearance is no match for the heightened intensity of energy of their special connection.

The new couple may be found at a gathering with friends or family. The intensity of their connection has them profoundly aware of each other even across a crowded room. Their shared smiles and looks bring an aliveness in their hearts and spirits just by the quality of feelings and attention they share. For the couple, the whole event and others in the room can take on an increased awareness, along with a feeling of aliveness in these connections.

What is the mystery that unfolds at these times when both people feel exceedingly alive and satisfied in the fascination of their shared time? I believe that it is not a complete mystery. Much of the beauty of it is simply the focused attention on their connection with each other and their surroundings. They are both fully present in the present moments.

And this is exactly the feeling each of us can create when we take the time to engage all of ourselves in moments while appreciating our surroundings, others, and the way we fit into them.

In other words, we can fall in love with the richness of our worlds just about any time. What wonderful gifts of joy, wonder, and mindfulness to give to ourselves.

FLIRTING WITH LIFE ITSELF

On the topic of romantic love, I was also pondering the idea of flirting. My friend Ann has oftentimes teased me saying that I am a natural-born flirt. So the time seemed to be right for me to understand how this talent might just be a gift of appreciating and engaging in the world around me.

Flirting means being playful, seeing the attractive qualities in others, and naturally enjoying life as it unfolds. But some of the interesting questions that occurred to me were: Can we expand the idea of what flirting is? Can it move beyond just an interaction with two people? Can you flirt with environments, individual moments, sounds, ideas, colors, tastes, textures, animals, movements in shapes, and all else life has to offer? What do you think? Can you?

Once I entertained the idea of flirting as a skill, I entered into a whole day of playfulness, curiosity, and amusement. Flirting seems to make many things eventful with simple recognitions. It is an interchange with energy at a deep level leading to finding oneself in communication with life itself.

When I say to myself, "I am flirting with life, as I engage in different moments," it brings with it an extra dose of good-natured lightheartedness and a feeling of a free-spirited dance of energy, awareness, and pure joy while truly finding myself a part of the adventure in the reciprocity in the moment.

When are some of the times you have felt robustly seen by the world around you while playfully interacting? It is important to explore how this "feeling seen" experience feels, and you can explore this feeling by being aware of how much you are present in your interactions with others, events, or objects. Really take some time to explore this thought.

Flirting can develop an increased depth of insight, gratitude, and boundaries. It is a choice in attitude and awareness. Can you sense the humor in a misshapen pumpkin in the fall; the brilliance illuminating around you from a light bulb while it explores the environment; the wonder in a puppy wagging its tail while scampering towards you; the warmth and tenderness of a well-loved blanket or pillow that comforts you? Flirting can enliven the abundance of endless, good-natured interchanges.

These feelings are like having a secret language with each chosen experience. You become a sculptor in the communication with all that is around you. It actually feels like a natural state of seeing and sensing expansive depths of exploration.

The idea of flirting is easily recognized when talking about two people who find themselves attracted to each other like the examples above. They may find their back-and-forth interchanges leave them both feeling fully alive by feeling seen, understood, and appreciated. This transformation into an altered connection is a state of wonder and alchemy.

Another example of flirting with the world is the anticipation of holidays, special events, or surprises and the feelings they can bring. You are actually dealing with an idea of the spirit of an upcoming event or one of a surprise. This example of anticipating a special event helped me to further understand the idea of engaging with our world, allowing me to be fully aware of feeling a part of an event by flirting with the ideas of sheer delight and anticipation.

I found the state of flirting to be quite simple, once examined. First, simply and genuinely smile. Next, follow this with lively engaged eyes directed towards the desired interaction. Then, notice your heart trustingly open to the curiosity as you figuratively step into an exchange of communicating while utilizing your five senses. Throw in measures of love, respect, exploration, and imagination. It is a gentle allowing through seeing, experiencing, questioning, and appreciating.

For me, at first glance, the idea of being fully aware and appreciating moments seems somewhat the same as flirting with experiences in moments. But on the other hand, when I use the idea of flirting in the richness of a moment, it brings an added interchange of energy which includes finding myself a dynamic player in the unfolding of words and emotions in this communication.

Flirting can appear in wide ranges of experience—from quietness to literally dancing in the moments. The liveliness is enhanced by putting oneself out there to create the magic in the exchange. Again, it's a choice to genuinely smile and open your heart to enjoying the abundance in the present. Everything around me seems almost new when I am captivated in this lighthearted way. My memories seem richer when pondering connections. Flirting with moments is a choice in awareness. This can be a learned skill or can be an innate gift which carries with it a touch of whimsical curiosity and depth of interactions. Let me give examples of what I mean:

1. You might touch a picture frame while full-heartedly pondering what tree it came from, who crafted it, how it resonates with the picture within the frame, feeling the shape, and conjuring up a possible journey it took to be at one's house.

2. With shapes, try exploring the curve of your shoulder, the feel of its strength, and remembering how it has supported you. What emotions come up for you?

3. Just the feel of chewing, and how your tongue dances in movements, or how your teeth feel when they come together is an adventure.

4. How about the sheer joy of just being able to walk, or even to move your arms—appreciation for what's usually taken for granted, like one's physical abilities.

Many captivating exchanges can arise from the alchemy of curiosity and appreciation, while fully engaging yourself— flirting—in this equation that leads to an abundance of unlimited involvements.

Entering this realm of artistry in flirting with the world around you is actually quite easy once you develop the skill. For some it may just take several minutes now that you have the formula. For others it may take a bit longer. I am still playing with this idea and am amused by the charm and romance of possibilities.

One such adventure happened on a sunny fall day while I was sitting with my friend Ann—the one who teases me about being a flirt—on her back porch. I was explaining how I had been playing with various ideas of flirting. I suggested we try it with a stately old tree in her backyard that was covered with hundreds of vibrant, bright yellow leaves, compliments of Jack Frost, I'm sure.

We focused on the grandeur of the tree, its farreaching sturdy branches, and the brilliance of the layers and layers of golden leaves which have graced Ann's backyard for years. With our intentions of flirting with open hearts, smiles, and acknowledgements, we found the connection with the tree intensified, and we felt very alive in the reciprocity of aliveness in the moment.

As Ann turned back towards me, I looked up and witnessed about 50 leaves falling from the tree all at once. With hurried excitement, I encouraged Ann to turn quickly around. As I was explaining what I had seen, another magical wave of leaves came tumbling from the branches like they were nodding to us in acknowledgement.

While we were still looking at the leaf -laden tree, wondering about the timeliness of these falling gifts of autumn, another dance of merriment greeted us with swirling leaves playfully descending on the carpet of green grass below. At this point, Ann said, "Oh please, I just want to enjoy the spectacular beauty of the leaves on the tree for many more days!"

The leaves stopped falling. We looked at each other and wondered about this perfect timing. We still smile about this seemingly magical exchange with the world around us.

Allowing an increased awareness can not only open you up to the beauty of depth in exchanges, but it can also bring in the importance of feeling where boundaries may be necessary, wise, or desired.

Let's say you are working with this idea of smiling and opening your heart to different situations, and you spy a spider merrily spinning in midair while in the act of creating an intricate web. You may react the way I did when I came upon this scene, when I backed up and inwardly shouted, "No way, I don't want to be totally open to the idea of spiders!" This led me to the idea that this way of flirting can lead us to being more fully aware of the feelings when needing or wanting to set boundaries. I could appreciate the spider and the scene, but a clear boundary popped up in terms of my heart not wanting to open in the same way; although, I could still respect the ingenuity of the spider and its creative world.

Flirting with the world around us is a skill waiting to be explored, developed, and expanded. It is there for anyone; it is a heartfelt choice away. It's a dance of aliveness with the enchantment and richness of all that is around us. All this beauty, humor, and charm is awaiting our attention.

A beginning list of the advantages of flirting with the world:

1. Enhances memory
2. Heightens appreciation, including the ingenuity and diversity in life

3. Develops skills of analyzing and assessment
4. Expands imagination and creativity
5. Fine-tunes likes and dislikes
6. Increases playfulness and lightheartedness
7. Broadens a sense of self and connections
8. Challenges us intellectually

NATURAL AWARENESS IN TIME

The Deer

An example of being pulled into a fully aware moment happened as I was working on this section of this book. I looked up just in time to see, out of the dining room windows, seven beautiful deer running across my backyard. They were escorted by a forceful wind while they dodged the wildly dancing Aspen trees. It seemed this strong, bold wind was foretelling of the snow and colder temperatures it was carrying along as a gift of the season.

In that moment, I could have returned to my writing. But instead, I chose to take a minute to really be present with that herd of deer and be a part of the gift of the magical scene. For just a few brief moments, I was in and around all that movement and liveliness. How radiantly expansive and alive I felt!

It would be lovely to capture moments like this one in a notebook titled Mindfulness in Moments. Journaling is an excellent way to support the idea of being aware in moments in our engagements, while preserving them to be recalled and enjoyed at other times.

The Charm of Awareness—Shining Lights

My friend and editor, Elaine, told me a beautiful story about a practice she had in her life when her two children were growing up. She was aware that the hecticness of the week, with the kids in school and homework and after-school activities along with her own work and her husband's long work days, often made her feel overwhelmed and wanting to withdraw from interacting with her family. In order to keep her connection to each person in her family, she did something special every Friday night. Either before or after dinner on Friday, when everyone was a little more relaxed because it was the end of the work week, Elaine, unbeknownst to the others, would gaze at each person, one by one, until all the week's stories and conflicts, sadnesses, and disappointments would fall away and all she could feel was loving appreciation for the person she was looking at. She says she would gaze at each one until all she saw was a shining light of their greatest selves. And when she saw this beautiful light, she could feel herself be that light too, and happiness was all around her. What a gift she gave to her children and husband each week. What a gift she gave to herself. And all without saying a word! And I just know that her children and husband felt that shift in energy.

Take several moments and think about people in your life, young and old. What are your connections like with them? How do you feel when spending time with each of them? What makes the time special? Are there things you might change or add to these relationships? Keep these questions in your mind as you read through the next pages. Have fun with this challenge.

Examples of memorable times I can easily recall with my children or grand-children are seemingly simple moments that stay gently in my heart. The feeling of holding their little hands in mine, seeing their angelic faces demonstrating their joys, frustrations, fears, and just plain anger always makes my heart smile. Hearing their laughter or seeing their little eyes well up with tears still brings with these memories many endearing feelings of awareness in the charm of these simple heartfelt moments.

APPRECIATING YOURSELF—CHANGING PLACES

Try this tool for richer and more interesting ways of connecting with one's self. It is spirited and refreshing. You know the stories about changing places—when two people have their consciousness switched and they end up in each other's bodies. There are many movies made with this storyline. Well, I came up with the idea of jumping into my own life for a day.

Pretend you are an outsider jumping into your own life and body. With this experiment you will find yourself discovering all sorts of possibilities: gratitude, amazement, sense of freedom, delight, and respect. The list goes on and on.

I found myself being so alive in this experiment for a day and a half when I tried this adventure. I kept hearing myself think, "Wow, I get to live this life right now."

Try it for any length of time; it is worth the exploration. For me, it was the idea of being completely immersed in life, and it just happened to be my life.

You can start right now where you are at: Close your eyes, make the intention of jumping into this intriguing game, and let the exploration begin. Savor the smallest detail. "Wow, I'm sitting in this cozy room in my favorite chair and reading this book." Look around at all the details in the room. Is anyone else in the house? You might be saying things to yourself like, "I get to enjoy and be a part of these winsome people's lives." If you take a shower, look around and truly enjoy your favorite soap, the idea you have hot water, familiar towels, and so on. Now go to the closet and drawers. Look at them as though this is the first time you've seen everything, and engage in how divine it is to get to use it. Notice: colors, smells, textures, etc. If there is something else that would make this exploration more alive, create it. The sky is the limit!

Light a candle, turn on some music, dance in the kitchen. Remember to really look with an appreciative, creative spirit without judgement. "This is so captivating; I am living this life."

Walk around your own home, and delight in what you have inspired and created. Explore and allow the different feelings and emotions to billow like gentle breezes into your awareness. Feel the peacefulness, connections, and memories.

If you have a pet, take the time to sit on the floor with it or hold it in your hands or arms. Really stop and allow the depth and gratitude of having this beautiful, bountiful creature in your life and heart.

Play the game of savoring while you explore your journey with the food you get to eat.

Continuing on, slow down, and with ease and anticipation, make each of your observations an event. Include even simple happenings, like being able to get up from a chair and being able to walk across a room to hugging someone special in your life.

Look down at your hands, feel the energy and durability of this body which has supported you this far. Look in awe. All the time remembering you are just borrowing this body and you are a visitor in this world.

This may seem like a silly idea, but if you do it, you may find it to be a new tool to use that is informative and insightful. I've been experimenting with it and have found it gives me a deeper appreciation in my life. It turns the ordinary into the extraordinary.

Jumping Into Movies

One of the things I started doing is pretending that I'm jumping into movies. Don't start laughing until you have tried it. This is much like jumping into books that I've described earlier. I pretend to jump into different scenes like placing myself in a car, either next to someone or in the backseat, while observing more closely what they look like. What does the interior of the car feel like? Touch the leather on the seats or smell the tobacco smoke. Is there perfume in the air? What feelings arise as you feel the intensity of the music? It is amazing what you can cook up. I may place myself on the sidewalk with the extras and really activate all five senses coupled with a bit of imagination. Before you cross this off your list, try it a few times. You could be standing at the top of the Empire State Building or sitting on a beach on a tropical island. Try watching something like an Indiana Jones movie; I dare you to jump into one of these rich dramas. This active level of amusement may be an avenue for increasing your creativity and involvement in the present moment. Once you practice jumping in on your own, it is easy to jump in and invite a child along!

The Pleasure of Experiencing Words

While developing the simple word list in Chapter 11, I discovered, purely by accident, as I kept glancing back and forth over this expanding list of descriptive words, that the most astonishing, and unexpected outcomes started happening. Because the majority of the meanings of these words are positive and strong, they started affecting how I was feeling in the present. I was surprised when these inspiring feelings, like breaths of fresh air, passed through me. It's like a playful and meaningful challenge to bring these qualities further into my life. I have found, by reading them with my full attention, the delight in their gifts are varied and abundant.

If you would like to engage in this experiment, you can make a list of your own words or add to the list in this book. Skim through the list in about three or four minutes maybe once a day for a week while gently thinking about the words and what they might mean to you. Try it different times when you are in different moods. Don't push for outcomes; just enjoy the journey. Look for clues in how they are touching or inspiring you.

CHAPTER 18

ADDING MINDFULNESS TO YOUR LIFE—
AT A TIME (Notes on Mindfulness Part 2)

This whole book is essentially about being fully aware in the moment in order to be present and supportive with the children in our lives, with ourselves, and with others. When we are fully present, moments are infinite. Of utmost importance is learning that we have choices in the tone and quality of our responses in those moments. This recognition is a gift we give to ourselves. Moments can be ordinary times, but it is the quality of our awareness that increases the insight into their richness. I'm not saying all situations in our lives are happy or without stress—of course not. But we can fortify our strengths by being increasingly grounded and centered in maneuvering through what life hands us.

Our culture has more expectations, distractions, and pressures than ever before. Oftentimes our lives are so busy it feels like we can't slow down. I think many of us are in a "fight or flight" rush as we go through our busy days with the numbing, adrenaline rush of demands. Have we learned to be attentively engaged or have we learned to be desensitized and distant as we walk through our many experiences?

Recognizing and understanding the demands in our lives is healthy, but the idea of it can seem almost frightening to us if we open the Pandora's box of naming and coming face-to-face with these intensities.

See if any of these statements resonate with you:

"I like the ability to be able to shut a lot of it out. If I didn't, I would really be completely overloaded. It almost feels like I wouldn't be able to do anything."

"I have so much to do, I need to move though my days almost on autopilot. If I stop, let's say, in mid-air, I feel like I could crash."

"I don't see an end in sight to the projects, commitments, and pressures."

With a practice of mindfulness, I suggest that you can learn to decrease the pressure that these hectic times bring and instead create a new spaciousness. Your unconscious self can and will begin to dance to this new tune, on this new dance floor, if you give it a chance. This quote, attributed to S. A. Jefferson-Wright, speaks to this quality: "Serenity is not freedom from the storm, but peace amid the storm."

CHANGING OUR AUTOMATIC RESPONSES USING AN UNEXPECTED GUIDE

So, how can this happen? How can you remember to bring in the infinity of the moment throughout your day?

With a bit of humor and sincerity, I hand you the idea of utilizing the wisdom of the "potty training" stages as a support in understanding how our nervous systems can be lovingly programmed for change.

Initially, babies and toddlers don't know they are wetting their pants. Then they start to become aware of wetting their pants after they are wet. They will probably start acting uncomfortable. Next, they become aware of wetting their pants while it is happening, but there isn't enough time to get to the bathroom. The toddler is interested in this happening, but not quite sure how to get to the bathroom on time like bigger people. Then they start to become aware, right before they start wetting. They will make it to the bathroom some of the time. Soon the toddler is aware and makes it to the bathroom with more regularity. They still like pats on the back for a good job. Final stage, the toddler no longer thinks about going to the bathroom; it is part of their day.

When we or our children are going through the stages of change, we need to be gentle and supportive with them and with ourselves. Having the knowledge that change can take time, choice, and perseverance is of comfort. Utilizing the wisdom of the potty training stages is a great example of how change can happen within ourselves for all sorts of adjustments we wish to make. Be sure to make friends with the frustration that can come with inconsistent progress. Because inconsistent progress is still progress!

Let's translate the "potty training" stages into stages of change that can be used more broadly.

First stage is to discover what it is you would like to change. Next is trying to catch yourself in this habit or way of being on a more regular basis. Awareness can be slow. Soon you will start to recognize it when it is happening, but not in time to usually change your response. Gradually, you will find your ability to influence change can happen with intention and thought, as the situation unfolds. This desired ability starts to happen on a more regular basis with less effort.

The ultimate treasure is when you look back one day and realize the change is happening without any real effort on your part most of the time. With a big smile, you realize your nervous system recognizes the change as the new norm or habit. Remember, these stages can go up and down and take time, even if the desire to change is strong.

ROADMAP TOWARDS FREEDOM

I like to think these next ideas are a roadmap towards freedom in our choices. How we fine-tune our awareness in moments in our lives is, of course, individual. But I invite you to try out my recipe. It might become a favorite of yours. I've divided it into five parts:

- Setting the intentions or tone when you wake up or go to sleep
- Creating one or more visualizations
- Bringing forth your own rich memories
- Learning to be more aware
- Recognizing your own special qualities on a regular basis

Freedom Recipe Part One: Intentions

It's supportive to start one's day with intentions. It can help set the tone for much of the day. When you wake up, is part of your normal routine to start thinking about everything there is to do and then reluctantly push yourself out of bed? Do you get ready in a routine fashion with the weight of a long list of responsibilities sitting on your shoulders? Is it like a heavy cloud which has you already starting your day in a numbed, rushed way? The cloud may be so familiar, you don't even acknowledge it.

A different possibility is fully choosing to take a few minutes that are truly yours. Try waking up with different morning rituals. Here are a few suggestions:

When you wake up and open your eyes, give yourself a gentle hug. Appreciate the blankets snuggled around you. Smile. Stretch your body like a cat testing its agility of movement for the day. When you get out of bed and open the curtains, greet the sunshine, rain, or snow with pleasant enthusiasm; really look and feel the grandeur of the day. You can say a prayer of greeting, perhaps tapping into your own specific religious or spiritual tradition. If time permits, add in five to ten minutes of stretching, like yoga or your favorite exercise routine. Consider topping it off with a thought for the day from a favorite book or calendar. Ask yourself, "Do I have an intention for the day or week?" If so, write that intention on a note card, and have it close at hand as a reminder. If you have a pet, consider adding in a couple of minutes of spending quality time with this pet. This will be a gift to yourself and your pet. Leave a note for a loved one, and in that moment feel the love you have for them. Maybe all you have time for is a genuine smile and a few thoughts of gratitude.

Pick and choose various ways of starting your mornings. This is a way to establish a feeling of peacefulness and joy that can follow you into the day.

Freedom Recipe Part Two: Creating a Visualization

As we have explored in this book, visualizing different environments can have powerful effects on the mind and spirit.

Create a visualization which brings a sense of support, vividness, and peacefulness. For example: maybe you see yourself at a lake. Really create the scene with the sounds of the water lightly lapping at the shore, birds singing, and chipmunks darting close by to see if you brought them some morning surprises. The smells of the woods and water, along with the feel of the moist air, brings a calmness to your being. Are you walking along the beach, sitting in the sand, and lazily creating designs, or are you leaning against a tree while watching a sunrise or sunset? Maybe there is a mother duck with her brood of fuzzy hatchlings comically diving and bouncing in the small incoming waves. Breathe into the quietness and peacefulness of the gift of the summer's day.

The more you can bring your five senses and emotions into your visualization, the stronger the feelings of contentment, joy, and wonder will be present. A calmness will encircle your heart. The richness of a visualization can be a way of bringing this calming awareness into moments throughout your day.

Spend some time internalizing your visualization. A good time to do this is at the end of your day, right before you fall asleep. Your subconscious will recall the quality of the calming feelings. The realness of these feelings will be one of your artist's tools for you to utilize when you need to reset the intensity when you are feeling rushed, overwhelmed, or numb. The feelings and reset can happen in a few seconds. It's as easy as taking a few slow breaths while recapturing the calming and quieting effects of your visualization as you gently breathe them into the present moment. The more you use this technique, the stronger it will become. You are choosing to change your habits in how you respond in moments.

Freedom Recipe Part Three: Snapshots

Adding to the creative endeavor in this recipe, you can find yourself enveloped in the stillness, realness, and wonder from earlier experiences in your life. These can simply be snapshots of various memories you have in your heart and mind. What makes these snapshots part of the quality in this recipe? Simple—the snapshots reflect the potency you felt when you were absorbed in them. In a lighthearted way, enfold the specialness of these encounters with others, events, or quiet times into your "now" moments, when needed. Savor the treasures of aliveness and warm support they continue to bring to you.

When my mom was in her early 80s, one snapshot I have of her was when she was washing a few dishes. She looked at me and stated pensively, "I don't know why I never liked washing dishes. It is actually quite relaxing and enjoyable."

The other time, I remember her looking out the kitchen window to the garage; there was a light on, which was unusual these days. She said, "It brings back so many memories of your father out there working on this or that. It is funny how a light can make you wish those days hadn't passed so quickly."

Freedom Recipe Part Four: Gratitude

Simply start to recognize and register gratitude towards the small things you do or the time you spend with others. You may not usually think about these things because they are routine, basically invisible. Make them visible with gratitude. Gratitude for family, health, friends, home, work, and community enriches the joy and appreciation of the now. In a lighthearted way, this helps to bring in an increased richness.

An example: Today I went to the bookstore with my husband, and with intention, I was really present with the depth of appreciation of just being with him, walking around the store while holding hands from time to time and exchanging thoughts. It truly felt like I was walking in a lovely, illuminated story of pure wonder.

Freedom Recipe Part Five: Recognition

Recognize some of your attributes that can bring a smile to your heart when you acknowledge them for yourself. Perhaps you acknowledge that you are: a loving parent; tenacious spirit; hardworking; excellent friend; generous, etc. This is an inside job—enjoy! I believe it is an important part of this recipe. I think many of us are oftentimes hard on ourselves, and this definitely reflects on the quality of our moments.

We can learn how to be increasingly aware of how we participate in the ups and downs in moments in our lives. The idea is for us to gain and refine a variety of positive internal responses that can be summoned in supporting us with a reassuring calm attentiveness. This art form of internal power and contentment is just an awareness and choice away.

You will be adding in your individual imaginations, experiences, and personality to this recipe. Remember, you are a beautiful force of nature. Smile, playfully and intelligently select your course for walking into your moments with more connection, aliveness, calmness, and insight. Be patient with yourself. This is like learning a new job. Enjoy the journey of the mind and spirit working together.

In summary, please stop, breathe, and enjoy the inspiring, quietness in your abilities and choices in how you spend your moments.

In giving honor to the power of imagination, and intentions, I would like to add this true story of Colonel George Robert Hall, who spent seven years as a prisoner of war during the Vietnam War. The story was reported by Charles Boatwright and featured on espygolfapp.com. Boatwright writes:

> "During these seven years, Colonel Hall mentally played golf in his confined cell. He memorized every aspect of each course he had played on, down to each hole, tree, rough area, fairway, and the speed of the greens. Every day he would mentally go through his routine until he was released on February 12, 1973…Upon Colonel Hall's release, the first thing he wanted to do was to play

his first round of golf. Within six weeks, he was invited to play in the 1973 Greater New Orleans P.O.W. Pro-Am Open, where he shot a 76, his handicap of (4)…Colonel Hall along with the other prisoners, were mentally and physically tortured, starved, and kept in solitary confinement. Colonel Hall's world consisted of a seven-and-a-half square foot cell, without basic necessities. The prisoners had little or no contact with the outside world or each other. The only lifeline the prisoners had was the virtual world they created in the theater of their minds."

This is an extreme example of a mind and a body under duress. But Colonel Hall's fascinating story gives us an excellent example of how even in more everyday situations we can use the superpower of our imaginations to enrich, change, and create in our own lives.

CHAPTER 19

IN SUMMARY: THE GIFT OF TIME

Spending quality time with children is one of life's treasures. These gifts of time are part of how we will influence who children become: how they feel about the world they live in, what they ultimately establish in their worlds as they evolve, and what children learn about the importance of quality, loving relationships.

We all know there are many variables that go into supporting children as they grow into adulthood: firm and loving boundaries, healthy food, varied experiences, involvement in activities, protection, honesty, consistency, positive reinforcement, humor, love, and laughter, to mention a few. But the gift of undivided time and quality in attention may very well be the most valuable gifts we can give to children, ourselves, and others. A lot goes into relationships, but the simple joys of spending time with another person where both parties feel appreciated, respected, and both delight in shared experiences is monumental. Children especially feel inspired, valued, and supported when they receive the gift of time and attention from someone who loves them.

May all your moments be infinite and all your time be blessed.

POSTCARDS FROM A LIFETIME OF MAGIC

Suzanne, my niece with two grown daughters

Here are a few of my memories with you, Aunt Linda, and Grandma Clara.

One weekend, when I was around five years old, Grandma decided she wanted to go crystal hunting in the mountains. Grandpa was unable to go with us, so, she decided just the two of us would go, which was rare since she seldom drove.

We hopped in the old Buick and headed to the gas station. This must have been "back when" unleaded gasoline was relatively new, because Grandma decided it would be best to use the super leaded gasoline. (Grandma would say, "If Grandpa had known we had spent the extra money, he would have been madder than a wet hen.") As we drove away from the gas station, grandma said, "Boy, that gas must be just like pure jet fuel, because this car feels like it is going to fly." The entire trip up the mountain we talked about how the car was racing and she could barely keep it under control.

Once we reached our destination on the mountainside along a beautiful stream, we stopped to search for crystals. Later, we realized we forgot to pack a lunch. Grandma said, "Who needs food when we have this delicious mountain fresh water?" We enjoyed the afternoon drinking out of the stream and digging in the dirt. And as Grandma would always say, "We survived the whole thing."

I don't recall if this adventure ended with a trip to the drive-thru in Lolo for a shake, but many of our outings did. Of course, now, there is a Dairy Queen in Lolo and I still have a hard time passing by it without stopping.

A couple of things we talked about today that I remember was Fred, my elf, and the bathroom window in your apartment. I also recall getting my first camera from Fred. I don't remember for sure if we tried capturing pictures of the elves or not because using film was much more expensive than taking pictures today. I imagine we may have tried to find at least a of few of them.

Also, I have the memory of hens and chicks (a succulent plant that has big growths surrounded by baby growths) growing in my little garden at Grandma's and, in the late spring, waiting for them to pop out. They definitely weren't one of the prettier things in the garden, but they seemed to multiply every year, and I acquired her love for them.

She would read her treasure books and then take armchair vacations with me next to her. We went on many an adventure during those times.

Besides crystal hunting, I also remember hunting for arrowheads by the riverbanks and the discussions about mountain lions. It always seemed a little dangerous because you never knew if one of those lions might just sneak up and grab one of us. She talked about her fear of them as a child living on the ranch, and how she felt that she surely was about to be eaten if one of them caught sight of her at night going to the outhouse. The way she talked about the screaming noise they made would have the hair standing up on both of our necks even in the middle of the sunny day on a mountain.

I have many memories of her finding treasures with her metal detector. I remember the story of when she had found about a total of $1.30 over a year with her metal detector. She made Grandpa report it on his income tax. Grandma said that Grandpa "sputtered about that one for a long time."

She really was able to find joy in the smallest things, and she found plenty of them. We always talked about the size of the ducks in the mud puddles during a rainstorm, the beauty of snowflakes, or the pot of gold at the end of the rainbows. We almost found this pot on several occasions, and would have, if it wouldn't have been for those sneaky leprechauns. There was always a lot of traditional magic on the holidays, too.

I did pass the magic and playfulness onto my girls. I named their elves: Mersadiez's elf is named George and Sierra's elf is named Clyde.

Madi, my granddaughter

"It's important to remember that we all have magic
inside us."

~ J.K. ROWLING

Mitzy found me when I was just five years old. I remember the
exact second that I first saw her, sitting outside on my Grandma's
porch, just waiting for a certain little girl to find her. I remember
sitting at the window and just watching her. Gorgeous, still, and
magical. I watched because I could not touch. For if I touched
her, it would cause her to fly away. I just wanted to take this
moment in for as long as I could. Eventually, I came away from
the window and when I came back, she was gone. Heartbroken,
I searched and found her, but not outside. Instead, she was
inside, sitting at the kitchen counter with a note. As I carefully
maneuvered around her beautiful pink and green dress, I found
the note wrapped in a beautiful, soft envelope, covered in rose
petals. I was taught to savor many things, experiences, and most
importantly I was taught to suspend moments in time and make
them last as long as possible. I exercised this ability at that very
moment; I wanted it to last forever.

After struggling through the note (as five-year-olds do), I found
out this fairy's name was Mitzy. She was very excited to come
live with me, but she couldn't show me magic because it was
against the rules. I was overfilled with joy. My very own fairy! I
had no idea that over time she would become my most trusted
confidante, my loyal adventurer, and even my inspiration to
travel and see the world.

First order of business was to ensure she was the most spoiled
fairy to ever exist. I proceeded to put out a bowl of blueberries
for her in case she was hungry and when Grandma and I came
back from our hike, the blueberries were gone! In my heart I truly
believed she was very much alive. I carried her around with me
everywhere, but only in the house. I wasn't ready to share her
just yet.

When my lovely trip at Grandma's house came to an end, I
packed up my things and went looking for Mitzy. I had made
her a very special seat in the back of the car right next to me. I
searched and searched, but I could not find her anywhere. I was
devastated. I had started to think she had flown off, not wanting
me after all, when I heard Grandma Linda yell, "Madi! Come
look on the porch!"

I flew to the front porch at lightning speed to find Mitzy sitting
there ready to go. I was, once again, overfilled with joy. She did
want to come home with me after all, and I hadn't lost her.

Over the years, I spent a lot of time with Mitzy. We talked and
played, shared secrets, and laughed a lot. She built me up to be
a smiling, joyful, and imaginative kid. When I had a hard day
at school, I would tell her about who hurt my feelings or a bad
grade I got. Not only was she a great listener, but she always told
me what to do. Along with my dad's humorous solutions, Mitzy
always taught me that kindness always won, and if I was sad, I
could call her to my shoulder and she would be there.

At that point in my life, she was there if I really needed her. It
was crucial that I had her to listen to me and give me advice. I
struggled with bullying and anxiety, and the person who could
calm me down or make me feel better was Mitzy. Although
I don't need her as much anymore, I still have that piece of
my life with me. She taught me patience, love, creativity, and
imagination. When we went on hikes, I saw fairy houses. When
I went outside, I tried to recreate those houses for the fairies,
and when I was hurt, I called my "gentle army" to my side and
they cheered me up. Even though I don't need the physical fairy,
Mitzy's spirit and lessons will stay with me forever for I would not
be here without them.

Ann & Coco, friends

My daughter Coco and I had the good fortune to be well
acquainted with Linda and her magical abilities with parents and
children. Coco grew up with Fred the Leprechaun and many fairy
families who visited our home and were secret friends to Coco.

St. Patrick's Day was a very exciting time in our house because Fred was a mischievous imp who came at night and tipped over chairs, scattered pillows on the floor, set wee traps for Coco, and left gold coins and TicTacs in his wake. Here are some of Coco's memories of growing up with Linda's magical touch, from her point of view:

1. Linda showed me some glowing paint on the ground and told me it was a whole other world that I could pop into.

2. Fred the Leprechaun was my friend even though I never actually got to see him. He had a home in a nearby forest during the summer and we would leave things for him to find.

3. Linda told me how the fairies lived in my piano, and they really liked it when I played. Sometimes they left little gifts if I practiced well!

4. One day, there was an envelope and a tiny statue of a fairy on a swing for me in my room because I had done something good.

5. I loved Fred, the leprechauns, and the fairies as I was growing up. I felt like I had secret friends that others didn't have. It felt like anything was possible and anything could happen.

6. Linda made it so fun growing up. She told me the secret that my toys and stuffed animals came alive when I left my room. This made it very exciting for me and I believed even more in this magical world.

Both of us benefitted greatly from Linda's light and playful magic wand of an imagination. As a parent, I couldn't have done it without Linda's encouragement, ideas, and engagement. We were extremely fortunate to have her in our lives. She reminded us that there truly is magic in our lives if we choose to see through the innocent eyes of our children.

Jessie Bean, my granddaughter

PLEASE NOTE: spelling and grammar are original to Jessie Bean.

There was a time when we had Grandma Linda over for the week. Grandma slept in my room. Every morning the fairies would come. They would bring hair clips, clothes, and other cool things. But one time like a month later Grandma came back and the fairies came and guess what they brought me? They brought me my very first fairy! I showed Grandma as fast as I could and Grandma said, "Look at that! It's very pretty. What are you going to name her?" I said, "I will tell you at the end of the day." So I thought and thought and thought some more, and finally it was the end of the day. I said I am going to name her Makayla. So me and Makayla played, and I also brought her to school. She flew on top of the car. We built a place in the back and named it Fairy Garden. I built a house for Makayla, and in the winter, I let her stay in my room. We had so much fun in Fairy Garden. We played games, and we had our cousin over. On Sunday, I looked up on my dresser and she was not there! I told Grandma in a frightened voice, "Grandma I can't find Makayla." Grandma said, "Maybe she is playing hide and go seek or she wants you to find her."

So what I did is I looked everywhere! I did not find her but I had not looked in my closet. And guess what I had found? I found Makayla! So, I ran up the stairs and I said, "Grandma, Grandma, look, look, I found Makayla!" Grandma said, "Good job, where was Makayla?" I said, "I found her in my closet." Grandma said, "That is amazing you could not find her sooner." Then, Grandma had to leave tomorrow. I got so sad, but she had to go home. Sunday came and it was time for Grandma to go home. She said, "I will come back in June," and in a blink of an eye it was June!

Once during summer it was time for Madi to go to Grandma's house. We met in Big Timber and Grandma and Grandpa got Madi and they said goodbye and headed off to Grandma's house. Every night I called Grandma and we flew to meet each other on something. I said, "I am going to fly on a butterfly that has beautiful wings that has diamonds on it and pink, blue, and purple around the sides." Grandma chose to fly on a purple penguin. We try to talk every single night but sometimes it doesn't work out. Grandma and Grandpa came over and they brought us Easter gifts. I got a jumper and a scratch out of horses, plus different shapes of chocolate. Madi had a soccer game, and so I wore my jumper and it was adorable.

After that, every night when Grandma was here, we watched a movie even if it's late. Then we jumped into our PJs and go straight to bed and wake up early. The fairies came again, and they brought some more fairies and more and more of them. I don't know how many fairies I have. If I counted them, it would take me all day. Also, if it wasn't late Grandma always told me a bunny story. She always gets ready for bed and when she gets out of the bathroom I am always sleeping.

Olivia, my granddaughter

Whenever I go to my grandparents' house, I immediately know that there is loads of fun waiting to come! Some of our favorite things to do are going to baseball games, the zoo, shopping, swimming, hiking, watching movies, and of course, garage sales. Every time that I go to Billings, I never want to leave! I usually go during the summer, when there is so much to do and I have the most free time to stay longer! If it were up to me, anytime I have a free weekend, I would say, "Let's go to Billings!" because I can't think of a better way to spend my free time than spending it with some of my favorite people of all time!

Jenny, my perfectly wonderful daughter-in-law

As my Mother-in-Law was working on writing her book, she asked me to write something in regards to what magic has done for my children. To be honest, I wasn't sure what to say. Magic was not part of my childhood as an only child, but I can remember using my imagination to make up games at my family's ranch to keep myself entertained.

In reflecting upon my children, though, I can say that magic has had a huge impact on their lives, and it's a gift that keeps on giving. Just the other day my youngest informed me that she would like to start leaving fairy presents for our neighbor across the street, to open up the possibility of magic in her life.

Magic makes the world a better place. I have enjoyed many hikes with my children, whether on vacation or in our own backyard, and enjoyed looking for fairy houses. When spring arrives, we talk about what the fairies are busy gathering. In our backyard, we have a space named Fairy Land, and it is a small wooded space where my children create magic and keep themselves entertained even now as 10- and 16-year-olds. It's a space that I do not tend, and they create different things, and sometimes I'm invited in to see what their imagination has created.

Magic opens up the possibility of what can happen. It's a lens that brightens my children's world and helps them to add kindness to the world and to others' lives. In life, as our children grow, a lot of what we as parents do is provide boundaries to keep them safe. Magic gives them a framework that is boundless. Magic is a gift that my Mother-in-Law gave to my children, and for that, I will be forever grateful.

Susan, a friend

It only takes a tale. The hot breath of deep summer washes over us. There's a lull in the play, a heavy settling of heat chains, making one lethargic and slow to think. A mother and five small children, we meander to the garden, stepping from stone to stone amongst the tomatoes and the asparagus fronds, hopping past the cucumber vines and the rhubarb, pausing under the grape vines for a bit of shade, watching the tiny shorts and tops waving on the line like many-colored flags. Again, the oven-like breeze moves our hair without cooling us. It's like…a dragon. And so it begins, the tale, the first tale: the saga of the dragon, a story of kidnap and recovery, of journey and danger. The epic adventure of rescue of those who need help, of perseverance in the face of discouragement, of bravery against the odds, of the courage of truth, of self-sacrifice not for the good of society but for the good of an individual, because nobody is expendable, and of the meaning of everyday choice—the decision to stand up to make things better or to draw back and protect oneself.

The tale has as many renditions as there are days it was told. And the heroes and captured shifted as often. It started as a way to pass the time, but it grew in nature. The stories came out of my own experience... not with dragons, but with stories made up around real people in my own mind. It dawned on me why I have told myself stories throughout my life, without really understanding myself. In all those stories, I bound up who I wanted to be, imagining circumstances that challenged those traits, and imagining persevering with my character intact.

As far as I can remember, it started with A Little Princess by Frances Hodgson Burnett, a delightful children's novel about a girl who never loses her integrity though her circumstances vary, which set me alight with imagination on a pathway to endeavor to do the same.

Medical technology has revealed that when a basketball player mentally pictures, say, shooting a layup, the exact same neurological pathways light up in the brain as when the action is performed. Much like an athlete who practices in real life and then goes through mental imaging to reinforce that muscle memory, I was practicing my character all the time. Now, armed with the power of story, I could subtly teach my children how to practice their character. I chose character traits I would love to see grow in my children: honesty, love of others, seeing the value in each person, bravery/courage (which I define as doing what is good, right, and true, no matter what), perseverance, integrity (which I define as being the same inside as out, among others as alone, undivided), and deliberate choice. There is a myriad of valuable character traits, and even more possible tales to tell and the value of telling ourselves stories can't really be overstated. The power to mold ourselves into who we aspire to be with integrity is priceless. Any of us can teach it, it only takes a tale.

FINAL NOTE: MORE MUSINGS OF JESSIE BEAN

Jessie Bean's Diary of a Week at Grandma's House

PLEASE NOTE: Spelling and grammar are original to Jessie Bean.

Hi guys it's me Jessie Bean.

Today's my birthday I'm turning 10 years old. I am getting so old. I got to go to my grandmas and gramps house at 1:00pm. I am so excited to see them. So, me and my mom went to the coffee pot and I ate a blueberry scone and my mom ate biscuits and gravy. When we went home and my mom took a nap and I went to go play with the twins. Then came home and packed and on my way to grandma's house. When we got to her house, we went garage sailing and grandpa took a nap. Then we went home and watched a movie. And as soon as you knew it was morning.

Every day I am going to try to write about my day. Today was a good day we went to the zoo and went to a Mexican place to eat lunch. At lunch there was a weird person that grandpa thought he was on drugs witch he probable was. So, what happened was the guy walks in and he sits down and he's looking at his menu and he starts waving it in the air and in my head I'm thinking boy he's crazy, and the waitress walks up and said "can I get you something to drink" and he just kind of stairs at her and she said something else that I couldn't understand and then he left. Then we came home and watched a movie. And now we are reading. Tonight, we are probably going to play games ride bikes and watch a movie.

August 13, 2019: We are going on a hike to pick huckleberries and there were only a few that we could pick on the bushes. After that grandpa said "Do you want to hike behind the waterfall?" And we said yes so, we went over some really big boulders. And as soon as you know it, we were there. The rocks were really wet and slippery. So, we stayed there for a few hours, then we headed back down and went to dinner. And came home and watched a movie and got ready for bed.

Today I hope all of you lovely people had the best day ever.

On the Pandemic

In the latter half of writing this book, the Covid pandemic of 2020 was raging across the world, and people were yearning for the adventures, freedoms, and engagements of their lives previous to Covid fears and restrictions. This led me to understand the importance of knowing or remembering how curiosity and the tenacity of desire in connection to our worlds can be just out our front door, in our back yards, or in our own homes. I love the fact that slowing down has created a deeper level in connections with others in our lives. I've seen more dads having time to walk with their children in neighborhoods, families playing more games, and cooking together. I believe it is human nature to try to make the best out of adversity.

On the phrase "Catching Diamonds"

The quality in the meaning behind the title phrase "Catching Diamonds" initially originated from a story in this book about my mom on a hot summer's day where she is catching diamonds from splashing waves. As Elaine, my editor stated, "I love the idea of how your mom turned the ordinary into the extraordinary!"

From here, we talked about how diamonds are considered priceless, and how their many facets dance with a creative aliveness that is revered and cherished by many. The uniqueness and clarity in diamonds can signify love, intrigue, and romance, to mention only a few. As the facets of the diamonds are carefully cut or lasered, the diamond's transformation reaches a preciseness in richness and magic in its ever-changeable radiance.

Aliveness, curiosity, and awareness in moments in our lives are much of what makes our hearts shine like finely cut diamonds while cultivating experiences in interests and engagements. These moments include quality time spent together while utilizing imagination, intentions, and connections while exploring with curiosity a variety of possibilities open to us in our worlds around us, with ourselves, and with others.

Thus, the phrase "Catching Diamonds" is there for anyone. Shake hands with the abundance of the worlds around you, and choose to find transformation in possibilities of delightful engagement in life itself.

What facets make your heart and spirit radiate in the clarity of wonder and play?

ACKNOWLEDGEMENTS

Many thanks to Elaine Silver, my editor; I am now privileged to count her as a dear friend in my life. Her touches of wisdom and encouragement, which have been added with a lightness and depth of intelligence, knowledge, and imagination, have beautifully enriched the unfolding of this book.

Thank you to my proofreader for this book, Natalie Korman. Natalie is a highly intelligent young woman with a discerning eye for the perfection and spirit of the written word and its interpretations. I love having her professional skills, as well as, her insightful heart being a part of this book.

Thank you to Eric Finsted for working with my husband Jim and creating such a beautiful cover that totally captures the spirit of the book.

Thank you to Carl Brune for the gorgeous and professional book design.

My husband, Jim has been a support over the years. I chuckle when I think of him patiently listening to me talk about fairies, elves, and the magic of imagination and adventures awaiting around many a corner. The addition of his artwork to support these ideas and the book cover are delightful. They will touch many a heart with smiles while evoking trips into fantasy and light-heartedness.

Others who have encouraged and supported me over time are world-renowned coach and friend, Ann Clancy. Beta readers: Michelle Pittack MS LCPC; Nora Flaherty Gray, grandmother, and English teacher; Jen Freeman, coach, Kathy Brayko, grandmother and teacher; Sarie Mackay, writer, and artist; Ben Carlman, therapist; Kate Barden, artist, mother, and grandmother; Jessica Cannon and James Kluz, new parents of Juniper; Camille Durbin, granddaughter of two wonderful grandmothers, and now a new mom herself. And thank you to Lindalee Hickey, teacher, grandmother and world traveler.

Thank you to Jenny Anderson, my wonderful daughter-in-law who has graced her children's lives with imagination and love in many diverse and creative moments. Thank you to a dear friend Juliana Hicks, who encircled me with delightful urgings in positivity in completing this book. And, of course, to my children, grandchildren, and niece, Suzanne, who are sprinkled throughout this book with love, adventures, and their charming imaginations and personalities.

ABOUT THE AUTHOR

LINDA COLLINS was born and grew up in Missoula, Montana, which is close to the mountains and many adventures. She graduated from Montana State University with a Bachelor's degree in Nursing, and spent the next five years working in the most restrictive youth psychiatric facility in Billings, Montana. Three of those years she ran a survivors' group. After divorcing when her children were young, she went back to school to get her Master's degree and Certification in Rehabilitation Counseling. The last 27 years she has worked as an RN Case Manager for the in-home Medicaid Waiver Program. These clients range from infants to the elderly with all manner of both physical and mental disabilities.

She still lives in Billings, Montana, where she met her husband, Jim Collins, in 1993. Their most favorite adventures include their children and five grandchildren who all live close by in Bozeman, Montana, except for one son who lives on the outskirts of Las Vegas, Nevada.

Linda hopes that as this book reaches diverse audiences, in all walks of life, it will bring increased positivity and inspiration to the possibilities of connection—in moments with children, adults, themselves, and life itself.

CPSIA information can be obtained
at www.ICGtesting.com
Printed in the USA
FSHW020104251021